What Others are Saying About *Farmhouse Devotions*

I spent my summers as a child on the farm, and many wonderful memories came flooding back while I read each devotion. Exceptionally well-written, *Farmhouse Devotions* is more than just a book. It invites us to see beyond the surface of our busy lives and discover God's divine presence. Cheryl will inspire you to pause, reflect, and praise our heavenly Father. His boundless love and grace are manifested in the simplest and most unexpected ways, and the stories are perfect analogies to the Word of God. I felt as if I was on the farm when I turned each page and felt the presence of the Lord. I will read this devotional again and again!

—Lee Ann Mancini
Founder of Raising Christian Kids
Author, Speaker, Podcast Host, Adjunct Professor, Executive Producer of Sea Kids

Farmhouse Devotions beautifully weaves imagery from everyday farmhouse life with deep and approachable spiritual truths. Cheryl's engaging storytelling will transport your mind past scenes from the Schuermann family farm to memories from your own life, reminding you of God's love and faithfulness and leading you to worship.

—Laurie Goree
MA in Educational Ministries
Co-Founder and Executive Director of Apollos Training International

Farmhouse Devotions is a captivating devotional that takes readers on a journey to the world in and around the author's family farmhouse.

Freshen and expand your perspective as Cheryl Schuermann reveals the joyful extraordinary found in the most ordinary things of life. See you at the farmhouse!

—Ava Pennington
Bible study teacher, speaker
Author of *Reflections on the Names of God*

From a walk near the pond to enjoying cracked, paper shell pecans to a view of the barn from a hill, Schuermann takes us vicariously to her farmhouse in sixty seemingly ordinary devotions with extraordinary and powerful messages. Through her words, the author reminds us to walk daily with Jesus, learning from Him and leaning on Him for support. Take a trip to the farm with Cheryl and draw closer to Jesus with each devotion.

—Julie Lavender
Raised on a farm
Author of *Strength for All Seasons* and *Prayers and Children's Bible Stories for Bedtime*

What do I think about my personal journey into *Farmhouse Devotions*? Three words come to mind: delightful, insightful, biblical. One truly feels privileged to visit the family farm with Cheryl as your guide. There are ample soul refreshments as she serves up practical life perspective from the inviting family pantry. On a regular basis, you will sense our Divine Creator, Rescuer, and Shepherd joining you on your visits to The Farm. I wholeheartedly invite you to come along for frequent soul-satisfying trips to The Farm with Cheryl.

—Bruce A. Hess, *ThM*
Pastor for forty-five years, Husband, Dad, Grandfather
National Speaker for FamilyLife Ministries (familylife.com)

CHERYL SCHUERMANN

Farmhouse Devotions

GOD'S GLORY IN THE ORDINARY

Farmhouse Devotions

God's Glory in the Ordinary

Cheryl Schuermann
Illustrated by Stan Schuermann

Kaleidoscope Publishing
Reflecting God's Truth

Farmhouse Devotions: God's Glory in the Ordinary by Cheryl Schuermann
Published by Kaleidoscope Publishing
1738 Oak Trail St. NE, Massillon, OH 44646

ISBN: 979-8-9893127-6-4 /979-8-9893127-7-1
Copyright © 2024 by Cheryl Schuermann
Cover design by Amber Weigand-Buckley – Barefaced Media. Edited by Shellie Arnold
Interior design by kae Creative Solutions
First edition editor Bold Vision Books team, second edition editors Shellie Arnold and Kristen Stieffel

Available in print from your local bookstore, online, or from the publisher at www.kaleidoscopebooks.net. For more information on this book and the author visit www.cherylschuermann.com

All rights reserved. Non-commercial interests may reproduce portions of this book without the express written permission of the publisher, provided the text does not exceed 500 words. When reproducing text from this book, include the following credit line: "Farmhouse Devotions: God's Glory in the Ordinary by Cheryl Schuermann published by Kaleidoscope Publishing. Used by permission."

Commercial interests: No part of this publication may be reproduced in any form, stored in a retrieval system, or transmitted in any form by any means—electronic, photocopy, recording, or otherwise—without prior written permission of the publisher, except as provided by the United States of America copyright law.

Unless otherwise marked Scripture quotations are taken from The Holy Bible, English Standard Version ®, (ESV®) Copyright © 2001 by Crossway, a publishing ministry of Good News Publishers. All rights reserved. ESV Text Edition: 2007

Scripture quotations marked (NLT) are taken from the Holy Bible, New Living Translation, copyright ©1996, 2004, 2015 by Tyndale House Foundation. Used by permission of Tyndale House Publishers, Carol Stream, Illinois 60188. All rights reserved.

Scripture quotations marked (NIV) are taken from the Holy Bible, New International Version®, NIV®. Copyright © 1973, 1978, 1984, 2011 by Biblica, Inc.™ Used by permission of Zondervan. All rights reserved worldwide. www.zondervan.com The "NIV" and "New International Version" are trademarks registered in the United States Patent and Trademark Office by Biblica, Inc.™

Scripture quotations marked (TLB) are taken from The Living Bible, copyright © 1971 by Tyndale House Foundation. Used by permission of Tyndale House Publishers, Carol Stream, Illinois 60188. All rights reserved.

Published in the United States of America

Dedication

For our parents, Ken and Alice Schuermann and John and Audrey Wilcox, who brought us the life-changing news of Jesus and left a legacy of faith, integrity, and love for the generations.

Table of Contents

Introduction		11
1.	Welcome	13
2.	Grafted In	16
3.	Redeemed	19
4.	Sticktights	22
5.	Renewal	25
6.	View From the Dock	28
7.	Weeds	30
8.	Prairie Flowers	33
9.	Quilts	35
10.	Tell Them	38
11.	Gather	41
12.	Secret Spring	45
13.	Entangled	48
14.	Broken Vessels	50
15.	Wings	53
16.	Seeds	55
17.	Faithfulness	58
18.	Landmark	61
19.	Sanctified	65
20.	Rain	67
21.	Pruning	70
22.	Bridge	73
23.	Preservation	76
24.	Seeking	78
25.	Relics	81
26.	Solitude	85
27.	Glass	88
28.	Jazz	90
29.	Story	92
30.	Pantry	95
31.	Stars	97

32.	Repurposed	100
33.	Treasures	103
34.	Laundry	106
35.	Campfire	109
36.	Image	112
37.	Roots	115
38.	Reflection	118
39.	Contentment	121
40.	Morning	125
41.	Walk	128
42.	Ordinary	131
43.	Washed	134
44.	Night	137
45.	Hope	140
46.	Rest	143
47.	Eagles	147
48.	Order	149
49.	Useful	152
50.	Perspective	154
51.	Unseen	157
52.	Heritage	159
53.	Stones	162
54.	Freedom	166
55.	Shade	169
56.	Maintenance	171
57.	Lost	173
58.	Grace	176
59.	Tethered	179
60.	Anticipation	182
In Closing		185
Recipes From the Farm		186
Notes		196
Acknowledgments		197
Meet Cheryl Schuermann		199

Introduction

In many ways, building the farmhouse was a spiritual experience. When I look back on the first turn of the soil in June 2016, God used the project to carry us through a time of grief. Over the previous five years, we said goodbye to all four of our parents. With their passing, we became the patriarch and matriarch of our family. A sobering reality.

Soon after Stan and I married in the early 1970s, his parents bought this land that we affectionately call The Farm. While the surrounding acreages are conducive to crops, the Schuermann land is unique with flowering meadows, deep rocky ravines, and a twenty-three-acre lake. The lake is magical with the best crappie and bass fishing in the area. One hundred fifty-five acres of playground.

Stan's parents had a vision for Stan, his brother, Rodger, and their families. Both Ken and Alice were raised in Oklahoma—Alice on a dairy and Ken on a wheat farm. They wanted their family to love the country in their discovery of God's created glory outdoors. Wherever their descendants lived in the years to come, they would always have this place to visit and enjoy.

All four of our boys first experienced The Farm as babies in a snuggly against our chests or riding in a carrier on our backs. They were rooted and grounded here. When they grew older, they explored, fished, built forts, and camped overnight—either in a tent or zipped into a sleeping bag in the bed of Grandpa's pickup truck. We built campfires and roasted hot dogs as the boys mastered a myriad of outdoor skills taught by their Boy Scout leader grandpa and Eagle Scout dad. From a young age, they knew this was a special place and a heritage to treasure.

Our sons grew into men, married, and began having children. They took their families to The Farm for hikes and fishing trips and picnics. We all dreamed about building a cabin—with a bathroom. The plans quickly grew from a cabin to a very large cabin to a turn-of-the-twentieth-century style farmhouse with enough space to hold all twenty-three of us at one time. We desired a style that captures the look and feel of our grandparents' era. Even more than this, we sought to create a place of rest, comfort, and adventure, where stories are discovered, and heritage is preserved. A place with a sense of belonging, discovery, and joyful work.

Every room of the farmhouse tells a story. Bunkrooms with vintage handmade quilts. Family history and old photographs hanging from picture rails. And a well-stocked pantry, providing a celebration of the old without neglecting modern conveniences. During construction, the family farmhouse motto was *Redeem. Restore. Repurpose.*

I became a regular at every antique mall and junk shop within a sixty-mile radius. Antique hardware, old doors, marble-topped washstands, and vintage furniture, most over one hundred years old, caught my eye. I took pictures of my finds, sent them to Stan, then asked the employees to "load them up." My SUV hauled a lot of history in those months.

Activities at The Farm flow from inside to outside and back again. I invite you to come along with me on this journey and enjoy God's glory in simple things. What we deem ordinary may be extraordinary, after all.

The Farm is open for you. Come join us!

1
Welcome

I am the door. If anyone enters by me, he will be saved and will go in and out and find pasture (John 10:9).

For several years, my father-in-law reminded Stan about the church doors he saved from the original First Methodist Church in Perry, Oklahoma. Besides being emotionally tied to the old building, my in-laws were from the generation that never wasted or threw away anything. They did not have a plan for the doors but believed everything could be useful one day. So, several decades-old doors made their way to the family farm.

Years later when my husband and sons cleaned the barn, the front doors to the old church emerged, complete with the original brass handles. Amid flying dust and cobwebs, we surveyed our treasures— dirty, coated with thick white paint, and missing some glass. We were thrilled to have them as the front doors for our new farmhouse.

Built in the 1920s, the doors were beautifully crafted to receive all who came seeking fellowship and words to sustain in times of trial. I imagine churchgoers sought God's wisdom in the church during The Great Depression. Farmers most likely prayed for relief from the devastation of the Dust Bowl in the 1930s. Mothers who had just said goodbye to their sons at the train station during World War II entered seeking God in prayer with tearful pleadings. From the most joyful events of a marriage to the most difficult goodbyes at a funeral, the doors gathered people in to receive words of encouragement and hope. Even now, the comfort and call are the same as times past.

When we enter doors, we seek what is behind them. Whether anticipating an all-you-can-eat buffet, a once-in-a-lifetime shoe sale, or the latest, greatest movie release, we go through the door to experience what is inside. Most of the time, this experience is temporary. But Jesus offers us something greater in the blessings of abundant life now and eternal life with Him in the age to come.

Jesus says He is *the* door, the way of entrance, and promises those who enter in through Him will be saved. By entering through Jesus, we can enjoy His presence and draw on His power. We enter by asking. "Ask, and it will be given to you; seek, and you will find; knock, and it will be opened to you" (Matthew 7:7).

Through this door, we enter the fellowship of believers and a generous storehouse of promises. When we go out into the world, Jesus directs us in bearing witness to the truth, ministering to others, and inviting them to the door. He will not leave us as sheep without a shepherd. All those who enter through Jesus, the Good Shepherd, will find pasture. No other access will take us there.

It is all here. Every blessing comes through Jesus to those who believe.

Welcome! Come and learn of the One who is the way to life eternal.

Dear Jesus, thank you that salvation is found in you, and you welcome me into your presence. Amen.

2
Grafted In

Whoever abides in me and I in him, he it is that bears much fruit, for apart from me you can do nothing (John 15:5).

My father-in-law, Ken, pointed to a tall tree in the middle of the clearing. "You see that pecan tree over there?"

How could I miss it? Rising more than eighty feet, the tree commanded the entire clearing, standing proud and majestic.

"Well," he continued, "it has a story."

I'm not sure if Ken forgot how often he shared this tale with me. Or, if he loved the story so much, it was worth retelling. Either way, I delighted in hearing it again. And again.

According to Ken, many years prior, the fruit was not worthy of the tree. The small, rock-hard native pecans were nearly impossible to open. Once cracked, a wrestling match was required to extract the meat.

The effort made the task time-consuming and hardly worthwhile. He invited a pecan tree expert from a local university to visit The Farm and evaluate the tree's potential.

"A graft is the only way to get better pecans," the man said.

After researching how to graft trees with a foreign branch, Ken cut a few branches from a friend's healthy paper shell pecan tree and proceeded with the surgery. The procedure took, and within a couple of years, the tree changed. It became a new tree, a new creation, nourished by the established root. It began to produce desirable fruit.

In Romans 11:17-24, the apostle Paul compares Israel to a cultivated olive tree and Gentiles to the branches of a wild olive tree. Branches of the wild olive tree were grafted onto the cultivated tree and received nourishment from the rich roots. In this way, Jews and Gentiles were brought together in God's family as one church, all partakers of the same roots, blessings, and inheritance. The promise God gave to Abraham of righteousness through faith is the same promise given to the Gentiles.

Because we tend to become arrogant, this good news came with a warning. Romans 11:18 says, "Do not be arrogant … remember it is not you who support the root, but the root that supports you." We did not save ourselves, and we're unable to sustain ourselves without God's mercy.

Rejoice. God saved you in His mercy and now supports you with His rich roots. The cut pecan branches Ken used for the graft had potential and the right DNA. But without being connected to the proper nutrients and sustaining resources, the branch could not produce fruit.

Our Father has taken us from a separated and unfruitful way of life and grafted us into His Son and His church. Jesus Christ is the very source of life of the tree and in Him we are a new creation. He provides us with the nourishment we need to bear eternal fruit for God's glory and to bless others.

Heavenly Father, thank you for bringing me into your family and making me a new creation. Thank you for providing me with the nourishment I need to bear spiritual fruit for your glory. Amen.

3
Redeemed

> The Lord your God is in your midst, a mighty
> one who will save; he will rejoice over you with
> gladness; he will quiet you by his love; he will
> exult over you with loud singing
> (Zephaniah 3:17).

Our son pointed to several two by six boards next to the barn. "Dad, where did this wood come from?"

"From the dump."

"Are they the same boards I threw away a week ago?"

Stan grinned. "Yes, the same."

Stan believes every piece of wood has potential. Beside the lumber lay a giant redwood beam, twenty feet long, that he found floating in the lake. Discarded and useless in the water, Stan figured it came from an old bridge and was worthy of being rescued. So, he used the loader bucket to do just that.

While building and furnishing the farmhouse, we operated under the motto: *Redeem. Restore. Repurpose.* We delighted in finding discarded items with the goal of redeeming them and making them useful again. Though often hard work, the result was worth the effort: the 1922 laundry sink, rescued from the old plumbing parts graveyard; turn-of-the-century doors headed to the dump; and too many items to list from junk stores. A desire to redeem is natural to us.

A clear and beautiful picture of human redemption is told in the Book of Ruth in the story of Ruth and Boaz. Ruth, a widow, worked in the fields of Boaz, a wealthy landowner, to feed herself and her widowed mother-in-law, Naomi. In Ruth 3:9, Boaz asked her name and Ruth's answer included a request. "I am Ruth, your servant. Spread your wings over your servant, for you are a redeemer."

Under Mosaic Law, a kinsman-redeemer was a male relative who had the responsibility to act on behalf of another relative who was in trouble, danger, or in need. His mission was to rescue and restore. To be a kinsman-redeemer, the relative had to meet four requirements. He had to be (1) related, (2) willing to help, (3) able to help, and (4) able to pay the price in full.

Ruth knew the law and approached Boaz as a relative. After she asked Boaz for mercy, he pursued the legal process of becoming the kinsman-redeemer for Ruth and Naomi. We see God's hand working through this tender story. When reading Ruth 4, we have no doubt of the great blessing born from Ruth and Boaz' union. Their son, Obed, became the grandfather to King David, in the lineage of Jesus Christ.

Generations later, God sent the ultimate kinsman-redeemer, His son Jesus. At His birth, Jesus became our brother. He was both willing and able to be the redeemer for us, even to death on the cross. Through His death and resurrection, He paid the price in full.

Our God redeems and rescues. With tenderness, love, and kindness, He bends down to us to quiet and comfort His people. Zephaniah 3:17 says He rejoices and exults over us with singing. Have you ever thought of the God of the universe singing over us?

God delights to love His redeemed.

Dear Jesus, You are my kinsman-redeemer. May I never forget the gift I have been given. Thank you for rescuing me and restoring me to my Father. Amen.

4
Sticktights

And they recognized that they had been with Jesus (Acts 4:13b).

Several grandchildren stood before me on the front porch, laughing and chattering about their big adventure. Sticktights, pesky barbed seeds, covered their tennis shoes and pant legs—God's version of Velcro.

"Where have you been? Wait … don't tell me." I knew exactly where they had been. The evidence was all over them. Patches of sticktight plants grew at the base of the horse corral. Obviously, the children had been with our horse, Jazz. They'd stood at the fence to pet him and left with new embellishments to their clothing.

In Acts 4, the apostles Peter and John were recognized as having been with Jesus. The evidence was clear. Luke records their arrest in Jerusalem. They were guilty of "teaching the people and proclaiming in Jesus the resurrection from the dead" (Acts 4:2). Peter spoke to the council, describing who Jesus is and declaring salvation is in no one else. When the leaders saw the boldness of Peter and John, the Scripture says, "they recognized that they had been with Jesus" (Acts 4:13).

Peter and John had boldness in what they knew to be true about Jesus. This knowledge was not merely hearsay, they were physically with Him. The disciples did not shrink back from owning their faith and, because they knew Jesus, they did not fear other men.

Imagine how much the disciples learned from three years with the Son of God. They listened to His teaching, heard Jesus pray, and observed Him interacting with others. They saw Jesus heal the sick. They knew Him. Knowing Jesus as they did, the disciples naturally wanted to imitate Him. Ephesians 5:1 tells us to "Be imitators of God, as beloved children." The disciples were blessed to have the Son of God to imitate, the perfect human being, the One who reveals the Father.

Being with Jesus is possible for us all. Though He is not physically with us in body, we have His Spirit and His Word. The more time we spend with Jesus through reading and prayer, the more we will become like Him.

Will others recognize where we have been? Will they see in us a loving spirit, kindness, holiness, and, yes, boldness? Just as the sticktights revealed where the children played, we should desire to have the image of God "stuck" all over us. Oh, that others would declare, "Ah, I can see the evidence of where you have been. You have been with Jesus."

Dear Lord, help me to embrace your Word every day so others will know I have been with you. May others see your truth "stuck" all over me. Amen.

Gratitude is a lifestyle. A hard-fought, grace-infused, biblical lifestyle.

-Nancy Leigh DeMoss

5
Renewal

Create in me a clean heart, O God, and renew
a right spirit within me
(Psalm 51:10).

When Stan and I walked into the junk store, we did not expect to meet a shirtless, shoeless man named Seven. I told him we were on the hunt for antique escutcheons and doorknobs. Without saying a word, he reached under a table and pulled out an old, rusty bucket. He dumped the corroded doorknobs and metal door plates onto the dirty concrete floor. "There ya go."

Most junk stores like this one have a guard dog hanging around. Not this place. Hearing a sound behind me, I turned to see an over-sized, beady-eyed rooster standing in the middle of the aisle a few feet away. When I took a step back, he took two steps toward me.

Stay," I whispered.

"Aw, he won't hurt 'cha," Seven said and turned and walked away.

Stan and I carefully sifted through the ugly, corroded, metal hardware, knowing the tedious work of scrubbing and polishing lay ahead. After selecting dozens we thought had potential, we paid for our treasures, while keeping a keen eye on Seven's junkyard rooster.

The process of cleaning the hardware came with a downside. Scrubbing more than fifty doorknobs and escutcheons with steel wool destroyed any semblance of our fingernails. But we had a plan for the hardware's renewal, to bring all the pieces back to their glory days and make them useful again. They were far too beautiful to live in a rusty old bucket.

Like we did with the tarnished hardware, God gathers us up from our lost state with a plan for our renewal. We are His chosen treasures. God promises to remove the stain, sand the rough edges, and transform us into something right and beautiful.

When King David cried out to God in Psalm 51, he requested a clean heart, knowing the one he had needed to be replaced. David recognized his sin and declared in verse 3, "For I know my transgressions, and my sin is ever before me." While David's personal weaknesses loomed large before him, he used them as the impetus to pray sincerely to God for help. He beseeched the Lord to purge his heart of unholiness and to continue teaching him wisdom in his innermost being. David desired to leave his failures behind and rejoice in the Lord.

God renews His chosen treasures, no matter their condition. In His presence, you will be restored and experience joy and gladness. You are God's image bearer. 2 Corinthians 5:17 says, "Therefore, if anyone is in Christ, he is a new creation. The old has passed away; behold, the new has come." Ask God to create a clean heart in you, renew your spirit, and make you like new.

Dear Lord, save me from my tarnished state and create a clean heart in me. Restore to me the joy of my salvation and give me an obedient spirit. Make me like new and show me how to walk as your image bearer. Amen.

6
View From the Dock

> Ascribe to the Lord the glory due his name;
> worship the Lord in the splendor of holiness
> (Psalm 29:2).

Have you ever stood before a scene that literally took your breath away? And you were certain you beheld something extraordinary? I experienced such a moment the evening I walked to our decades-old pontoon boat-turned-boat-dock to await the sunset. The setting of the sun over the pond did not disappoint. The still water provided the perfect canvas for the glory God would soon display. As the sun's light transformed the clouds above, the reflection shimmered on the water below.

I wanted desperately to stop time, to touch the golden reflection on the water, and to capture the image in my mind for a bit longer, knowing I would never again see it exactly like this. I felt very small and could do nothing to add to or take away from the scene in front of me. My task was to sit on my plastic ice chest and behold it—and snap cell phone pictures of the constantly changing sight.

Since that glorious sunset, we have marveled at many more and have often wondered what to do with this beauty.

Beauty in itself does not satisfy. If we look upon a spectacular sunrise or sunset or the view from a mountaintop to give us peace, meaning, and purpose, we will be disappointed. Nothing other than knowing the God who created the wonder we behold can ultimately satisfy these needs.

God created us to be spectators of this world and prepares these scenes for us to enjoy. Gazing on such sights should take us straight to the Creator in humility. This is the worship God desires from those He created. Even in God's display of glory, we know His greatest delight is in us. For here, we see God's spirit in creation and in our recreation. Now *that* is a wonder.

While we marvel at the beauty around us, God and all the angelic realms behold us as redeemed saints and marvel at *our* beauty. "As for the saints in the land, they are the excellent ones, in whom is all my delight" (Psalm 16:3). We who once were rebels and not at all delightful are now made beautiful by grace.

When we experience a glorious scene at the beach, a mountain peak, or in our own back yard, let's marvel at God's creativity. Praise Him and give thanks. Be bold in declaring, "The heavens declare the glory of God, and the sky above proclaims his handiwork" (Psalm 19:1). Be filled with wonder at the display of God's creative glory which shows forth in us, His redeemed.

Dear Father, when I see displays of your glory and power, I want the experience to change me. I know you see me in your Son and delight in me. Teach me how to humble myself before you and give you all the praise. Amen.

7
Weeds

Put to death therefore what is earthly in you
(Colossians 3:5).

"Where did these weeds come from?" I stood on the porch surveying the front lawn, hands on my hips in defiance. "I mean it. Who planted them?

Unfortunately, the natural tendency of soil is to produce native grasses and weeds. Their seeds are indigenous to the earth and were there long before we put down Bermuda sod. Our front lawn alone probably harbors millions of undesirable seeds waiting in the soil for the opportune time to sprout and take over. When the conditions are right, they will emerge.

Early in our marriage, many years before we built the farmhouse, Stan and I lived about thirty minutes from the family land. We wanted to plant a garden and thought The Farm was the perfect location. Stan plowed the soil in our chosen plot and raked the fertile ground into rows.

Anticipating a bountiful harvest, we planted hundreds of seeds—yellow squash, zucchini, okra, and green beans. With no way to water our garden, we trusted the rain would come and make it flourish.

It did rain and the magic happened, but not as we envisioned. When we returned to the vegetable plot a week or two later, weeds were thriving, and we spent several hours pulling them out so our delicate seedlings could grow.

The next time we arrived to tend our garden, we discovered the weeds were again winning. They were so tall we could not find the vegetable plants. Every good plant was entangled and choked out by the unwanted bandits. The weeds that easily gave up their position two weeks before, now dared us as they stood nearly eyeball high. They were opportunists and quickly took advantage of our distraction, inattentiveness, and basic neglect. The good plants needed daily attention and we failed to care for them. They did not give us even one green bean.

Sin is as natural to man as weeds are to the soil. When left unchecked, ugly thoughts and the resulting behaviors such as discontentment and grumbling proliferate, just as those unchecked weeds multiply in our lawns and in our gardens. Do you ever feel the weeds in your life are choking out the spiritual fruit you try to cultivate? Just as the desirable things of earth must be cared for and nurtured, the desirable parts of our lives must be cared for.

Friends, be encouraged as you spend time in God's Word, in sweet fellowship with Christian friends, and listening to the wise teaching of trusted theologians. In Titus 3:14, the apostle Paul instructed Titus to make sure the Christians whom he ministered to were devoting themselves to good deeds, so they wouldn't be unfruitful. He didn't say, "Make sure they have one more thing to do." He wanted them to focus on the good.

Let's be diligent to cultivate the good things in our life, so worldliness will not have the nutrients it needs to prosper.

Heavenly Father, thank you for granting me the tools I need to be a good gardener. May I not grow weary of tending to my own garden and producing good fruit for your kingdom. Amen.

8
Prairie Flowers

> Why are you anxious about clothing? Consider
> the lilies of the field, how they grow: they
> neither toil nor spin, yet I tell you, even Solomon
> in all his glory was not arrayed like one of these
> (Matthew 6:28-29).

Every June, before the man comes to mow and bale the meadows, Stan and I embark on a wildflower tour around the farm property. We take special notice of the variety of flowers God placed in our chunk of prairie. Some blend in with a host of like flowers; some stand tall and dominate above the rest. A few beckon to be touched while others dare us with their prickly spikes.

As we examine the flowers more carefully, we recognize how God arrayed each one with its own grace. Each is uniquely provided for. A meadow full of purple lemon beebalm, black-eyed Susan and prairie fleabane complement the bright orange of the Indian paintbrush. A closer look might reveal deep purple winecup clarkia, delicate cup-shaped flowers that often take on the color of red wine.

We can learn a lesson from these beauties. In the Sermon on the Mount, Jesus uses the way God has arrayed flowers with such glory to illustrate His provision for us. He knows we are prone to anxiety and worry, and how hard it is for us to avoid them.

Anxiety. Worry. They overtake us and pull us down, and we struggle to get out from under them. According to Jesus, being anxious will not help us in any way, not even to extend our life by one hour (Matthew 6:27). But God, the Creator of the wildflowers, will not forget His beloved.

If God takes such care of flowers that are here today and gone tomorrow, will He not take care of us, His eternal children and heirs to His kingdom? Jesus tells us not even Solomon in all his glory was arrayed as these flowers. Though diverse in color, texture, and size, wildflowers in the field have one thing in common. They reach for the sun, trying to find their place where they can receive the life-giving light. The flowers breaking through to the sun will grow strong, while those unable to do so will be stunted.

The next time you are greeted by beautiful flowers, lay your worry and anxiety aside and reach for the Son, the Lord Jesus Christ. Believe God when He tells us: "Humble yourselves, therefore, under the mighty hand of God so that at the proper time he may exalt you, casting all your anxieties on him, because he cares for you" (1 Peter 5:6-7).

Dear Father, I want to be concerned with the right things, the important issues of this life, and leave the management to you. Grant me the faith to trust you for material things and to be satisfied. Amen.

9
Quilts

In my Father's house are many rooms. If it were not so, would I have told you that I go to prepare a place for you? (John 14:2).

During the farmhouse planning phase, we enjoyed thinking about every possible combination of people who might be our guests—children, adults, singles, couples. Besides our family and friends, our vision for the farmhouse included occasionally hosting ministry leadership retreats. We wanted our guests to feel as if we had prepared the farmhouse just for them.

The house plan included five adult bedrooms plus two bunkrooms, one for girls and one for boys. Preparing the bunkrooms for our grandchildren and guests brought us a lot of joy. The bunkrooms each have three sets of bunkbeds and one full bed. Stan and one of our sons built the bunks. The full bed frames are estate sale finds.

As soon as we finalized the design, I went on the hunt for vintage quilts. Nothing says cozy like an old quilt. A friend gave us three quilt tops from her grandmother and another friend finished them for me. Every single stitch and detail of the tops were sewn by hand, a tapestry of love.

To locate the remaining quilts, I waded into the world of online auctions, winning some and losing some. Over a few months, the acquired quilts were finished, repaired, washed, and ready for guests. Gathering fourteen vintage quilts and quilt tops took time but the result is just what we hoped for: comfortable and cozy.

How comforting to know Jesus Christ prepares a place for us beyond life on earth. In John 13 and 14, John details the events of the Last Supper where Jesus tells the disciples of His imminent parting. Some were sad, others were discouraged, and all were frightened. Jesus told them one would betray Him, and all would fall away (Matthew 26:31). He comforted them as we comfort young children when we say, "I'll be back for you soon." Jesus said, "Let not your hearts be troubled" (John 14:1).

Jesus told the disciples His heavenly home had many rooms, and He was preparing a place for them. When He shared this, they could not envision the millions upon millions of people from every tribe and nation and tongue coming together in one household to live with Jesus. He will have ample room for all who come to Him. He will not run out of accommodation in the place where every need is anticipated and planned for.

While we work to provide comfortable temporary accommodations for our guests, Jesus is preparing an eternal dwelling place for His church that is far more than we can imagine. In Ephesians 2:7, the apostle Paul says Christ will "show the immeasurable riches of his grace in kindness toward us." In heaven, we will experience peace, joy, and rest forever with Christ.

Dear Lord, my heart can't begin to imagine what you have prepared for me in heaven. Thank you for making ready a place for me where I will dwell with you forever. Amen.

10
Tell Them

> Tell it to your children, and let your children tell it to their children, and their children to the next generation (Joel 1:3 NIV).

Ah, the joys of living in the country. The season of the wasps. The invasion of the gnats. Swarms of ladybugs that manage to get into the farmhouse and have their reunion along the baseboards. And the grasshoppers. It seems as if we are always reminding the children to close the doors behind them.

At a certain time of year, small worms crawl up onto the porch. Not harmful, but annoying. Last year, a brief hatch of teeny, tiny bugs covered the outside door frames. Thousands and thousands of them. Even with a magnifying glass, we could only determine they were not no-see-ems; they were hardly-see-ems.

When entering the farmhouse through the front doors, guests are greeted by a large gold frame, a garage sale find. Though the frame is ornate, the message from Joel 1:3 is simple and powerful. It reads: "Tell it to your children, and let your children tell it to their children, and their children to the next generation."

Here, the prophet Joel describes a devastating invasion of locusts as a result of the people's unbelief. Far worse than any minor critter annoyances we experience at The Farm, the swarms of locusts could destroy an entire food supply and leave a nation hungry. An economic disaster and dangerous health crisis. Joel calls his people to obey God.

This verse is our farmhouse theme. Though we don't describe plagues of locusts to our children and grandchildren, God instructs us throughout Scripture to teach them about His sovereign rule and power. Joel 1:3 is a constant reminder of our desire to infuse the family with such a love and reverence for God that it carries on from one generation to another.

The honor of being the "grand" patriarch and matriarch brings ample opportunity to continue investing in our family. The blessing of grandchildren also comes with a great commission. In Deuteronomy 4:9 (NIV) God solemnly instructs the Hebrews through Moses to "Teach them (God's statutes) to your children and to their children after them."

This could not be more clear. Grandparents are called to a grand work—to be two-generation teachers. Psalm 145:4 says, "One generation shall commend your works to another, and shall declare your mighty acts." In Exodus 3:15, God tells Moses, "This is my name forever, and thus I am to be remembered throughout all generations."

Making God real to our children and grandchildren begins at the family hearth. We want our children to observe us standing strong in the face of adversity. We want them to see us trusting the God who overrules all the events of our lives in His kindness and mercy.

Throughout the Bible, we're reminded to remember God and His works and promises and pass them on. Let's commit to being the historians in our homes, sharing the stories of God's provision and the atoning work of Jesus Christ with our family.

Dear Lord, may my family see evidence of my increasing love for you. Help me keep the gospel alive in our home and may it be a living testimony from generation to generation. Amen.

11
Gather

A new commandment I give to you, that you love one another: just as I have loved you, you also are to love one another (John 13:34).

Whenever our family gathers, the entire flock ends up in the kitchen—the big sheep and the little lambs. Sometimes small dogs lie down under the island. Occasionally, a big dog runs inside through the front door and heads to the back kitchen door with a couple of kids in hot pursuit. Observers may call it mayhem. We call it fun. Cooking and food prep happen in the midst of it all, and everyone talks at once.

When designing the farmhouse kitchen, we knew we needed a large island because no matter the size of a kitchen, everyone shows up there at the same time.

"How big?" Stan asked.

"As big as you can make it."

"Okay. Nine feet long big enough?"

I shook my head. "No."

Stan built the island nine feet long, the longest that could fit in the space. For this project, he used yellow pine for the top and leftover porch posts for the legs. He added two outlets underneath the island top for the pancake griddle and an occasional crock pot of chili.

Gatherings at the farm are treasured times, and the bigger the gathering, the better. When the food is ready, someone calls people in from the yard and the porches. The favorite method to call for dinner is to clang the triangle or shake the cow bell and yell, "Dinner!" At some point in their development, the children learned to wait until they were outside to do this. When everyone is gathered in with hands washed, they remove their hats, and we circle up to pray and sing "The Doxology." "Praise God from whom all blessings flow."

After Jesus's resurrection and ascension, God created the church as the body of Christ. Though the church was made up of individual members, they were charged to be united in focus. They were to carry each other's burdens (Galatians 6:2) and rejoice and mourn with each other (Romans 12:15). We are called to do life together, side by side.

God intended for humans to interact with humans, whether we're sitting around a living room or a kitchen island. He made us for relationship. Hebrews 10:24-25 says, "And let us consider how to stir up one another to love and good works, not neglecting to meet together, as is the habit of some, but encouraging one another, and all the more as you see the Day drawing near." God intended for us to build something together.

As ideal as this sounds, being in community and dwelling in unity takes effort and is not always easy. In fact, it is rarely simple. Still, the apostle Paul charges us to make every effort to let love be genuine and to live peaceably with all (Romans 12:8, 18). Gather your flock and embrace the opportunity to be with others as God intended.

Dear Lord, give me a genuine love for others and show me how to extend that love with a tender heart and a humble mind. Amen.

Trusting God means looking beyond what we can see to what God sees.

-Charles F. Stanley

12
Secret Spring

> Those who drink the water I give will never be
> thirsty again. It becomes a fresh, bubbling
> spring within them, giving them eternal life
> (John 4:14 NLT).

While much of the land surrounding The Farm lacks a readily accessible source of water, we are blessed with a twenty-three-acre reservoir, man-made in 1963. To our delight, the reservoir known as Black Bear #71 is one of the best fishing ponds around. But for some of our grandchildren, the Secret Spring is the most magical water feature on the land. When I asked one of the girls why it was so special, she whispered, "It's hidden."

The day the children took me to see the Secret Spring, one of my granddaughters held my hand and told me to close my eyes. "Trust me, Grammy. I'll lead you there."

In years past, I visited some springs in neighboring Arkansas. With a turn of a spigot installed in a rock wall, you can fill an empty milk jug in seconds with clean, spring water. When I opened my eyes at the Secret Spring, the picture was quite different.

I stood at the edge of a small pool of water with rocks rising on the opposite side.

Water trickled out of a crack in the rocks and dripped into the pool below. Green moss grew around the small opening, indicating a constant state of moisture. A tiny flower bloomed in the moss, causing me to smile. Though small and seemingly insignificant, this source of water from an unlikely place delighted the eyes and tickled the imagination. The Secret Spring *is* special, and it's available to all.

When the Samaritan woman sought water at Jacob's well in Sychar (John 4), she was surprised when a Jewish man spoke to her and asked for a drink. Jews did not associate with Samaritans, so she questioned him. Jesus ignored her question and said, "If you knew the gift of God, and who it is that is saying to you, 'Give me a drink,' you would have asked him, and he would have given you living water" (John 4:10). The woman merely sought temporary relief from her thirst, knowing she would have to return the following day. What water did this man speak of? She did not understand how it could satisfy her thirst.

The woman had no knowledge of Christ, and this lack caused her spiritual thirst. She could fill herself with water from the well, but it would not satisfy for long. Only the living water from Jesus would give her eternal satisfaction and life. His words were life-giving, living water. Revelation 22:17 says, "And let the one who is thirsty come; let the one who desires take the water of life without price." Jesus wants no payment. If we are willing, we are invited to drink. All come in the same way, and all will be refreshed.

If you desire this living water, trust Jesus and accept His invitation. Jesus said, "I am the way, and the truth, and the life. No one comes to the Father except through me" (John 14:6).

Take His hand. Allow Him to lead you to the spring of living water and to a life fulfilled and abundant in every way.

Dear Lord, you promise to give me a spring of water that will well up within me to eternal life. Your words are life-giving truth. Amen.

13
Entangled

Let us throw off everything that hinders and the sin that so easily entangles (Hebrews 12:1 NIV).

At The Farm, we have many reasons for urging people to stay on the paths. It's possible to encounter a snake, friendly or otherwise, during certain seasons. Then there are those uninvited pests who like to attach to us, like ticks and chiggers. The need to stay on the path is most important in the spring and summer, while winter is the safest time to venture into the woods. Anytime of the year, the likelihood of an encounter with danger is far less if we remain in the safe lanes.

Without a threat of snakes, ticks, and chiggers, we might think a winter hike off the trail would be carefree. But it rarely is. Briars and thorny vines grow just off the trails. The thorns are long and sharp, and the vines form a tangled net, ready to capture anyone who ventures into their domain.

The vines seem to have a life of their own, entangling those who walk too close. If we aren't prepared—in the words of our son, Matt, when he was a young boy—we can get "stucker and stucker." Often, the only way to get from here to there along the path is to carry large hedge clippers, cutting our way through as we go. Sounds like a scary jungle, but it isn't. Just untamed Oklahoma woods.

This scenario is much like our own existence. We live in a world where it is easy to become ensnared with a host of distractions and sins. Arrogance, falsehood, unforgiveness, even worry come to mind. Unless we cut free, one sin can lead to more, and we soon find ourselves captured.

In his letter to the Hebrews, the author tells us we are to fix our eyes on Jesus. "And let us run with endurance the race that is set before us, looking to Jesus, the founder and perfecter of our faith" (Hebrews 12:1-2). This ensures we will not only stay on the path, but we will stay out of the distraction-filled woods. On the path, the entanglements will be easier to identify and remove before they snag us.

God has set a race before us, and it is one we must run. It is not a race we can choose to sit out, for there is no safe place of leisure where we can be idle. The enemy of our progress never slumbers.

Follow hard after Jesus, and He will never fail you. He will keep you safe and on the path. Remember, He *is* the path. Proverbs 4:25-26 (NIV) says, "Let your eyes look straight ahead; fix your gaze directly before you. Give careful thought to the paths for your feet and be steadfast in all your ways."

If you find yourself entangled in the cares and worries of this world, or falling into sin and getting stucker and stucker, look up. Fix your eyes on Jesus, the perfecter of your faith.

Dear Jesus, I want to keep my eyes fixed on you. Your words are true. I will trust you, the perfecter of my faith. Amen.

14
Broken Vessels

He heals the brokenhearted and binds up their wounds (Psalm 147:3).

Snoop around the outside of any old, abandoned homestead or barn, and you will find pieces of broken glass bottles and ceramic dishes, tossed away when they were no longer useful.

My dad would have had a field day at The Farm. I called him the King of Super Glue. He certainly thought he was the best around at fixing broken things. And since he broke something nearly every day, he was afforded lots of practice. Whenever I caught him peeling bits of dried glue from his fingers, I knew he had recently tackled another repair. Before long, I would surely discover his latest project—a dinner plate, vase, or a ceramic figurine. "Good as new," he'd say. "No one will ever know."

In fifteenth century Japan, artists created kintsugi, a method of incorporating art into the repair of broken pottery. Meaning "joining with gold," kintsugi embraces the beauty of flaws and imperfections and treats breakage and repair as part of the history of an object. When a vessel is damaged, it is repaired in a way that highlights and emphasizes the cracks, often with liquid gold. Rather than being discarded, the object is restored, and the brokenness celebrated in the life of the object. Marks of wear and experience are valued.

The word *vessel* is used often in the Bible and denotes a flawed person whom the Lord calls and uses for His purposes. Seeing our own flaws generally causes degrees of guilt and discouragement. What use is a broken pot or a broken bottle? Thankfully, God does not see us this way. He sees us made new in Christ, healed, whole, and useful.

In Isaiah 61:4-6, God promises to restore the people and raise them up, and to repair the "devastations of many generations." Even if the destruction has occurred for decades and the walls are broken down, He will use His people to rebuild. They are set apart to serve the Lord. He promises to remain with those who are broken, bind up their wounds, and make them stronger than before.

Broken vessels have a story of mercy and restoration to tell. Though we may see ourselves as broken and worthy only of the junk pile, God sees us as valuable and useful. The more He uses us, the less we will focus on ourselves. No more shame. No more confusion. God intends to use us to bring His message to a broken and hurting world. Wherever God has us, that is the ideal place to serve Him. Recall how mightily God used Paul, the self-proclaimed chief of sinners, and Peter, who was famous for denying the Lord.

When you feel useless or broken in spirit, present yourself to the Master Potter. "The Lord is near to the brokenhearted and saves the crushed in spirit" (Psalm 34:18).

God chose you and knows what needs mending in your life. He is a God of restoration and wholeness. He is near, and you will find renewal in His hands.

Lord, I marvel at your mercy and am amazed you would use me, a broken vessel in need of restoration. Heal my wounds. Make me whole and useful for your purposes and glory. Amen.

15
Wings

> For his invisible attributes, namely, his eternal
> power and divine nature, have been clearly
> perceived, ever since the creation of the world,
> in the things that have been made
> (Romans 1:20).

The back porch is one of my favorite spaces at the farmhouse, because it invites me to relax, reflect, and pray. If I were a poet, this is where I would write verse. Instead, I watch hummingbirds.

For several months every year, hummingbirds buzz up to our feeders on the back porch. They sound like giant wasps while they hover, move forward and back, and from side to side. They fight with each other, drink for a few seconds, then zoom off into the woods.

These little winged wonders flutter their wings at a remarkable sixty to eighty times per second. Their wings do not flap—they rotate in a figure eight, making them even more extraordinary. This movement enables them to go backwards and to hover in one spot. And their hearts beat about 1,200 beats per minute. They are marvelous mini machines.

During the spring migration, hummingbirds arrive in Oklahoma in mid-March and early April. In September and October, they head to Central and South America for the winter. They know when to come and when to go. They know the appointed times without anyone telling them. And, miraculously, they know the way. Even the recently hatched babies somehow know.

God blessed us with a great variety of birds. He could have made all birds sparrows. Not to take anything away from sparrows, they are happy little birds. But if every bird were a sparrow, we would only hear chirps. We would never experience the caw, the hoot, or the gobble. We would miss the meadowlark's cheery song and the whippoorwill's nighttime greeting. We would not experience the stunning display of colorful plumage from the cardinal, the roseate spoonbill, the parrot, or the peacock.

All the intricate details of a bird's existence are intentional, and all function according to God's design and wisdom. When life seems confusing, observing God's hand in designing even the tiniest hummingbird should give us great assurance that He is in control. Every single thing that can be seen, touched, heard, and tasted in nature should cause our eyes to lift to the Creator himself.

God purposed to reveal His attributes in the world around us. When you observe the birds, do you have a sense of God's grace and mercy toward you? Do you grasp the power of His sovereignty? Stop and take note. Look with your eyes and listen with your ears. God has made himself visible in all of creation.

> *Dear Lord, I marvel at the spectacle of creation. I will see your hand and receive your grace in the beauty around me. Amen.*

16
Seeds

As for what was sown on good soil, this is the
one who hears the word and understands it.
He indeed bears fruit and yields, in one case
a hundredfold, in another sixty, and in
another thirty (Matthew 13:23).

At The Farm, we like to think of ourselves as farmers—though we only have one horse, some bales of hay, and around one-hundred needy pecan trees. We do love to plant various seeds. But just like a farmer, we must manage and work within the boundaries before us. As every farmer or gardener knows, the condition of the soil determines if the seed will sprout and the plant will grow. Before planting millet seed in the newly dug pond, Stan helped the soil by introducing organic matter—manure, donated by our horse. We call it Jazz Magic.

One of our favorite memories is when two of our sons taught their children how to sow seed in the prepared soil. The children lined up at one end of the dry pond then spaced out from side to side. They each carried a plastic cup of millet seed and tossed it out as evenly as possible while they walked. When all the seed was distributed, Andrew stood on a wooden pallet tied to the back of the truck. Daniel drove the truck slowly while Andrew rode the pallet like a surfboard, turning the soil to just cover the seed. Not exactly mom-approved, but it worked.

In Matthew 13, Jesus tells the parable of the sower, and the ways seeds can fail to take root because of the condition of the soil. Seeds falling on a path are vulnerable to the elements and are snatched up by birds. Seeds falling on rocky ground do not have the depth of good soil to take root.

In verse 22, Jesus talks about thorny ground, the example most Christians can relate to. Crops typically don't compete with thorns as much as weeds, but the point is seeds aren't alone in the furrow. Though the soil may be prepared, indigenous weeds compete with good seeds for the nutrients and the water.

Our lives are crowded with distractions and temptations. The demands of a phone that never stops ringing and dinging, and even ministry demands can choke out the good seed. We only have so many nutrients, and so much water, and so much space. Much of the Christian life involves cultivating good thoughts and making sure bad thoughts don't overspread the garden.

Your heart is like the soil. If it is conditioned and ready to receive God's life-giving words, it will be as good soil, hearing the Word and understanding it. Hold the words fast and allow them to take root. "Sow for yourselves righteousness; reap steadfast love; break up your fallow ground, for it is the time to seek the Lord, that he may come and rain righteousness upon you" (Hosea 10:12).

Give God's Word space to grow first in your mind, then in your actions. Be blessed with a rich harvest.

Dear Lord, I pray you will open my eyes to understand your words. I desire for my heart to be as good soil, ready to receive your truth and blessing. Amen.

17
Faithfulness

Well done, good and faithful servant. You have been faithful over a little; I will set you over much. Enter into the joy of your master (Matthew 25:23).

Occasionally, someone in town mentions to Stan that his mother taught them in Sunday school. They smile and Stan wonders if they were one of the ornery ones she had a special love for.

During the farmhouse construction, in one of the barns at The Farm, we found the door to her classroom hidden behind the grand entry doors and the chapel door from that same church. Alice's door was fairly unassuming. No glass, no distinctive details. When Stan pulled it into the light for closer examination, the foil stick-on letters and numbers told the story: Grades 3 & 4.

For nearly twenty-five years, my mother-in-law, Alice, taught third and fourth grade Sunday school in our small town. No large audiences.

No media coverage. No parades. She just quietly served the children who came.

Prior to opening the door for the children on Sunday mornings, Alice spent several hours preparing her lesson. She kept a prayer journal and prayed over each child who might come, possibly spending extra time on a few challenging souls. When they arrived, Alice greeted them by name, warmly welcoming them into the room. She could not know what God would do in the life of each child, but she believed He would use her preparation and kindness. Alice was always there, knowing she served her Lord by bringing these young hearts to Jesus.

We gave her classroom door a makeover, complete with a new finish and a brass plate stamped with vintage stamps: Grades 3 & 4. The door now has a prominent place in the downstairs hallway in the farmhouse, a constant reminder of a life lived with purpose and commitment. Only God knows how many children's lives were touched and how many accepted Jesus because of Alice's faithfulness.

In Matthew 25, Jesus tells the parable of the talents. In this story, He illustrates how servants used the gifts they received. When Jesus commends those who invested their gifts wisely, He praises them as good and faithful servants. When we think of the word *good*, the following often comes to mind: kindness, doing the right thing, selflessness, setting aside one's own desires to serve others. The word *faithful* implies continuance in obeying God's statutes, trusting Him for the outcomes. Servants joyfully do the bidding of their master. As a result, their day is oriented to the desires and heart of the one they serve.

God has given you gifts, and it is your joyful task to discover them. Peter tells us, "Each of you should use whatever gift you have received to serve others" (1 Peter 4:10 NIV). Look for ways to faithfully invest your gifts and ask God to make something beautiful and eternal for His glory. Ask Him to honor your faithfulness in the small things and give you joy as you do His work.

Dear Lord, direct my heart and efforts as I seek to follow you. Show me how to use gifts you have given me for your purposes. My desire is to hear you say to me, "Well done, good and faithful servant." Amen.

18
Landmark

For I the Lord do not change (Malachi 3:6).

Claire Rock, named after our granddaughter who discovered it, is a large rock formation protruding from the side of a hill in an untamed part of The Farm. Though seasons change around this massive rock, the rock itself does not change. The rock is well-established and has no doubt been there for thousands of years. A point of reference, it will remain as new generations come to explore.

Armed with a laminated trail map provided by an adventure-loving uncle, our young explorers often trek through the woods until they reach this established point of reference. In our family's version of orienteering, the children move from checkpoint to checkpoint, looking for markers that do not change. Large enough for several people to sit or stand on and survey the canyon below, Claire Rock beckons the hikers to pause and rest. Sometimes it is a destination, but often it is a beginning point for the next grand adventure.

This landmark tells the children where they are in relation to everything they will discover on The Farm. If the hikers strike out from the rock and find themselves lost, they can retrace their steps. All their destinations can be oriented to this unchanging reference point.

Throughout the Bible, we read stories of God's everlasting love and guidance. Jeremiah 31 tells of the Israelites' exile to Babylon. Jeremiah 31:21 (NIV) says, "Set up road signs; put up guideposts. Take note of the highway, the road that you take." God promised they would return one day to their own country. He urged them to build landmarks along the route, so they could later retrace their steps to find their way home and back to relationship with Him.

Every great awakening or reformation is a return to the eternal God who speaks to us through His unchanging Word. This is true of our own awakening. He is our point of reference and orients us to everything in our lives. He is consistent in provision. His character and eternal purposes remain. In Deuteronomy 32:4, Moses wrote, "The Rock, his work is perfect, for all his ways are justice. A God of faithfulness and without iniquity, just and upright is he." God is steadfast, strong, immovable; He is a refuge for those who need direction. Outside of His guidance lies confusion and the likelihood one will become lost.

Staying on the path is hard, especially when we have an adversary who likes to lure us away. He changes the signs and attempts to move us off the path. The journey to lostness usually begins with one step, one purposeful move away from the safety of the Rock.

If you ever feel lost and unsure of which way to turn, look for a landmark with substance. Though everything around us changes, we can be sure of the unchanging, solid Rock. Through every journey, God remains true and does not change. He is both our destination and our beginning point for the next adventure.

Dear Lord, you are my unchanging, solid Rock and landmark. Grant me the ability to orient everything in my life to you and your Word. Amen.

We will never find happiness by looking at our prayers, our deeds, or our feelings; it is what Jesus is, not what we are, that gives rest to the soul.

-**Charles H. Spurgeon**

19
Sanctified

Therefore, if anyone is in Christ, he is a new creation. The old has passed away; behold, the new has come (2 Corinthians 5:17).

When we decided to use only the buffet portion of an antique oak hutch in the dining area, the top became homeless. The three-foot- tall oak top piece was originally created with many pieces of wood, carefully fitted together like a puzzle. A beveled mirror set in the center, cloudy from age. Into the barn it went to live out its days with a variety of old, seemingly useless furniture.

One day, I mentioned to Stan I needed hooks for the guest bathroom. He looked thoughtful for a moment, then went rummaging in the barn. He found the hutch top and lifted it out of the pile. After disassembling it, Stan trimmed and refit the remaining pieces. The result was a stunning wall piece, complete with antique hooks. Not only did he make it visually pleasing, he made it good and useful once again.

Christians often talk about sanctification, the process of being remade to be more like Christ. The generic meaning of sanctification is *the state of proper functioning*. To sanctify someone or something is to set that person or thing apart for the use intended by the designer. The new bathroom wall piece was sanctified with help from Stan's creativity, a table saw, and some wood glue.

In the theological sense, a human being is sanctified when he or she lives according to God's design and purpose. This begins when the Spirit of God makes us a new creation. He chooses us for a unique purpose, sets us apart, and preserves us, His beloved ones, for good works.

In the High Priestly Prayer in John 17, Jesus pleads for those given to Him. In verse 17, Jesus says, "Sanctify them in the truth; your word is truth." The truth we need to grow, mature, and gain wisdom is found in the Word of God. His Word is the instrument of sanctification and cannot be neglected. When the doctrines of truth enter our hearts and take residence there, they will work to change us, to sanctify us for God's eternal purposes.

If we are willing to let God remake us, He will transform us into something beautiful. God will lift us out of our old way of life and remove what is no longer useful. The end result is we will be perfectly suited for our new purpose, for our new way of life in Christ Jesus. God, the designer, does the work by conforming us to the truth in His Word.

Dear Lord, thank you for saving me and setting me apart for your purposes. Make your truth come alive in my heart and sanctify me for your glory. Amen.

20
Rain

Do the skies themselves send down showers?
No, it is you, Lord our God. Therefore our hope
is in you, for you are the one who does all this
(Jeremiah 14:22 NIV).

When farmers get together, the topic of conversation always turns to rain. Will it rain too much? Will the rain come at the right time? Or will we get any at all?

After a bit of musing and grumbling, one of the farmers usually offers the encouragement, "It'll rain. It always does. Sooner or later."

Everything about farming revolves around the rain. A farmer knows the growth of his crops depends on what God does. The farmer can't make it rain, and he certainly can't create the soil. He has to work, focusing on what he *can* do, and continue to plant seeds.

One spring, Stan worked with a bulldozer operator to build three new ponds at The Farm. He wanted to not only attract waterfowl but to create some new fishing spots for the grandchildren. When the bulldozing was complete, several family volunteers planted millet in the freshly dug soil. Then, they waited and waited for the rain.

In Ezekiel 34:26, God says, "I will send down the showers in their season; they shall be showers of blessing." Who can say this except God? None of us can make it rain. Nor can we send showers of blessings from heaven. In this verse, God makes it clear He delights in being gracious to His people. He delights in showing mercy to us.

The prophet Isaiah declares: "Therefore the Lord waits to be gracious to you, and therefore he exalts himself to show mercy to you. For the Lord is a God of justice; blessed are all those who wait for him" (Isaiah 30:18).

Waiting is hard and can be discouraging. God says He will sustain us even amidst waiting. He will send down rain in its season and will bless us as we look to Him in obedience. Faith looks forward. But we must look back to the promises and help God has provided in times past.

In James 5:7, James assures us, "Be patient, therefore, brothers, until the coming of the Lord. See how the farmer waits for the precious fruit of the earth, being patient about it, until it receives the early and the late rains." The farmer may not know when the rain will come, but he can pray with confidence. God brought rains in the past and He has promised to bring them again. "It'll rain. It always does."

Knowing God's promises gives us confidence to trust Him for what we don't yet see. Are you experiencing a season of drought? Expect rain to come. Are you burdened with sadness? Then this is the season for showers. Our gracious Lord promises to bless us. Bow before Him and get ready for a heavy watering.

Dear Lord, grant me the faith to believe your Word, to believe your promises, and to confidently bring my requests to you. Amen.

21
Pruning

> Every branch in me that does not bear fruit he takes away, and every branch that does bear fruit he prunes, that it may bear more fruit (John 15:2).

Two pear trees stand in a back corner of the pecan grove. Years ago, when our boys were young, we collected pears from these trees—buckets and buckets of pears. Unfortunately, they are now unproductive, their branches entangled and fruitless. Though we know fruit trees must be pruned to produce fruit, life has a way of taking our attention and our energies elsewhere.

With other pressing needs on the land, these trees never made it to the top of the priority list. The only time we think about them is when we happen to walk past and say, "Oh, yeah. We really should prune those trees.

The pecan grove has a different story. From what we know about its history, the grove was originally planted with around one hundred fifty trees. Every tree was placed with an expectation of fruitfulness. But through the years a series of storms, including a devastating ice storm, left the grove in terrible shape, resembling something out of an apocalyptic movie set. Roughly half the branches of each tree lay on the ground. Not a pecan to be found anywhere.

This cleanup and pruning required sturdier tools than loppers. Like maybe a bulldozer? That is exactly what happened. Stan hired a man with a dozer to push over the badly damaged trees, uproot them, and shove them into a ravine, never to be seen again. The thinning had to be done. Then, he could come back with a chain saw and pole saw to prune the remaining trees.

Though the cutting back may seem drastic, the work of the pruner is always a work of love. His desire is to bring out the best by removing what is unwanted and detrimental. The best pruners are skilled, knowing what must be removed and taking care to remove only that which keeps the tree or branch from fruitfulness. To the observer, it may look like the tree is being harmed, but the pruner has a plan for enabling it to flourish. Thus, it performs according to its created purpose.

Have you ever thought *something needs to go*? Our life may need a trim or it may be ready for a bulldozer. When God prunes us, His desire is to bring out His best in us. God is careful to remove only the parts of our lives which inhibit our growth and fruitfulness.

At times, God might choose to remove something from our life for our protection. This may call for some heavy limb cutters, but God is ready to help us channel our energies into the most important areas. Though the pruning process may feel like adversity, He loves us enough to remove unhealthy attachments. Jesus said, "I am the vine; you are the branches. Whoever abides in me and I in him, he it is that bears much fruit, for apart from me you can do nothing" (John 15:5).

As the tree is subject to the arborist, so we are subject to the Master Pruner for His glory and our fruitfulness.

Dear Lord, show me how to yield to you, the Master Pruner. Remove unproductive attachments and relationships from my life and help me channel my energies into the most important areas. Amen.

22
Bridge

For there is one God, and there is one mediator between God and men, the man Christ Jesus (1 Timothy 2:5).

Who doesn't love to discover a wooden bridge tucked into the woods? If it looks sturdy enough, it beckons us to cross over, but not before we stop a moment, lean on the rail, and peer down at the creek. We have such a bridge at The Farm. We don't know its history, but it was obviously built to allow getting from one side of the creek to the other.

Several years ago, Stan determined the bridge was no longer reliable enough for vehicles and needed to be rebuilt. The base of the bridge is made of large stones, shaped to fit together like a puzzle and secured with mortar. They rise about twelve feet from the bedrock in the creek to support the beams of the bridge.

Though the rock foundation was secure, all the wood needed to be replaced. Our goal was to make the bridge strong, secure, and long-lasting.

For two days, Stan and his boys, young men at that time, strapped on tool belts and handled heavy wood beams and three-inch-thick planks. Soon, one side was no longer separated from the other. We could easily cross over.

Mankind has a similar "bridge problem." Our sin separates us from God (Romans 3:23). The chasm of our separation is deep, and we are unable to cross by ourselves. But God, because of His great love for us (Ephesians 2:4), sent His son to take us where we cannot go ourselves. The prophet Isaiah records when he saw the Lord in a vision (Isaiah 6:1-2) and experienced His glory. In an intercessory prayer in Isaiah 64:1-2, the prophet cries out to the Lord, pleading with Him to come to earth. "Oh that you would rend the heavens and come down, that the mountains might quake at your presence … to make your name known to your adversaries, and that the nations might tremble at your presence!"

The word *rend* means to rip or to tear open. Isaiah beseeched God that He would *tear open* the heavens and show Himself to the world. Because of the chasm separating man and his Creator, we need a mediator, an intermediary between a Holy God and sinful people.

God showed himself to the world in the person of Jesus Christ. In 1 Timothy 2:5, the apostle Paul makes clear there is only one God and one mediator between God and men. Jesus Christ is fully God and fully man (John 1:1-14). He is the mediator, the one who bridges the gap between heaven and earth, between an infinite God and finite man. Jesus does what we cannot do on our own. He is the only bridge to carry us safely over to salvation and eternal life.

As the bridge, Jesus will bear our weight. He is approachable and we can draw near to Him without fear. Though worldly influences never stop working on us, Jesus beckons us to come across.

We don't need tools or construction plans. We simply approach the bridge, listen to the One who beckons us across, and believe He is the only way to arrive safely on the other side.

Dear Lord, thank you that you came to earth in the person of Jesus Christ, providing a way for me to approach you as my Father. Thank you for carrying me safely across the bridge to salvation and eternal life. Amen.

23
Preservation

The words of the Lord are pure words, like silver refined in a furnace on the ground, purified seven times. You, O Lord, will keep them (Psalm 12:6-7).

From the 1700s through the 1940s, lath and plaster was the preferred method of constructing interior walls. Narrow strips of wood (laths) were nailed horizontally across the wall studs or ceiling joists, then coated in plaster. These walls were expensive to repair when damaged, so hanging wall art on them was risky.

Around 1840, Americans began using picture rails to hang art and mirrors in their homes. Set about an inch from the ceiling, the wood rails resembled molding. Specially designed metal hooks clipped neatly around the top of the rail to hold cords attached to framed art and pictures.

When we decided on an early 1900s style farmhouse, picture rails and copper hooks seemed ideal. And we loved the idea of not making holes in the walls. If we decide to move a piece of wall art, we lift it off the picture rail and move it down the hall or to another room. The walls remain untouched and their integrity is preserved. No more lines of holes in the sheetrock behind a wall hanging from a husband's search for that elusive stud.

In Psalm 12, King David declares confidence in God's ability to preserve the integrity of His own words for mankind. He says God will keep them through the centuries and guard them for the generations to come. Jesus said in Matthew 24:35, "Heaven and earth will pass away, but my words will not pass away." God preserves His words, and they will be with us through eternity. We have His wisdom at our fingertips. Even the very words He spoke when creating the heavens and the earth.

The words God spoke to Moses, and Abraham, and Mary the mother of Jesus, are available to us. We have the words Jesus spoke when He bade Peter and Andrew to follow him, when He healed the man born blind, when He chastised the Pharisees for their failure as shepherds. From the beginning, God's Word has been preserved for us.

Man attempts to preserve temporal things, but the farmhouse walls will eventually come down even without the presence of nail holes. God has preserved for us the eternal. His plan is for His Word to be preserved in our minds, so we will think and act biblically. God's Word is too valuable to be sitting in a box or on a coffee table, rarely opened. His words contain transforming power, so we may believe Jesus is the Christ, the Son of God, and that by believing, we may have life in His name (John 20:31).

Dear Lord, thank you for preserving me by your sustaining grace. Thank you for preserving the existence and the integrity of your words for mankind. May I be faithful to pass them on to future generations. Amen.

24
Seeking

> His divine power has granted to us all things that pertain to life and godliness, through the knowledge of him who called us to his own glory and excellence, by which he has granted to us his precious and very great promises (2 Peter 1:3-4).

"You know," Stan assured his grandson, "whatever you need is in the barn ... somewhere. All you have to do is find it."

The family has heard this many times. They roll their eyes and head to the barn to find what they're looking for. Folgers coffee cans full of lag screws, nails, washers, nuts, latches, and carriage bolts line shelves and rolling carts. Whatever they need is probably there amid the life jackets, fishing gear, hunting tubs, paints, solvents, and John Deere tractor ... somewhere. They just have to search for it.

Everything from my father-in-law's garages and sheds migrated to the barn. Some of the hardware and tools came from Stan's grandpa's farm in northern Oklahoma. Yes, they are turn-of-the twentieth century old, but Stan says they're still good and useful. During the farmhouse construction, the amount of stuff in the barn grew. Yet, we sometimes discover the building does not have every item we need for every task. Though well-supplied, its resources are limited, and a trip to the hardware store may be necessary.

In 2 Peter 1:3, Peter says God has granted to us all things we need for life. All things? A bold statement. God has granted us His "precious and very great promises." Everything we need for our journey through life can be found in His Word and our knowledge of who God is. We have no reason to look elsewhere.

When you experience sadness and grief, God promises comfort. Jesus assures you, "Blessed are those who mourn, for they shall be comforted" (Matthew 5:4).

If you are fearful, God promises to strengthen you and help you through whatever you face. Isaiah 41:10 (NIV) says, "Do not fear, for I am with you; do not be dismayed, for I am your God. I will strengthen you and help you; I will uphold you with my righteous right hand."

For the tired and weary, Jesus promises rest. "Come to me, all you who are weary and burdened, and I will give you rest" (Matthew 11:28 NIV).

Whether we seek wisdom in relationships, guidance for raising children, or assurance in times of doubt, let's place ourselves under the care of the One who wants what is best for us. How do we access His great storehouse? God promises to provide for us when we take our requests to Him in faith.

Though Stan's barn seems packed full, it does not contain everything. Nothing compares to God's Word for providing the encouragement, the instruction, and the hope you need. Armed with this confidence, dig into the vast storehouse of the Scriptures. You will find what you seek.

Dear Lord, everything I need can be found in my relationship with you. I confess my unbelief. I want to hide your Word in my heart and believe the many promises you have given me. Increase my faith so I can trust you more. Amen.

25
Relics

> Put off your old self, which belongs to your former manner of life ... Be renewed in the spirit of your minds ... Put on the new self (Ephesians 4:22-24).

The dump. Every farm has one or more. Our land is no different, and we discover areas of the property where the broken, discarded, and no longer wanted were tossed through the decades. Though many of the small items are covered with dirt, a heavy rain may cause them to resurface. When an old spark plug emerged from the ground, a little research revealed it was from a car built in 1928.

Fragments of pottery and glass not visible yesterday might lay in the dirt today, now only partially buried. With a little effort and searching, we could fill a box with rusty hinges and latches and whatchamacallits, as my grandmother would say. While the larger relics remain hidden under the ground, the small things tend to be exposed, to reveal themselves as they come to the surface.

We typically do not go looking for anything useful in the dump of discarded things. They are simply relics and reminders of a past life. They show themselves when disrupted.

For the Christian, old attitudes, old hurts, and thoughts we assumed were long gone tend to emerge when something triggers their return. Pieces of our former lives reveal themselves. At that point, we have two choices. We can adorn ourselves with the old relics, or we can put on something new.

Unfortunately, old sins and addictions are just under the surface, and the right conditions can easily bring them up. When we think we have put an old sin to rest only to have it resurface, we should remember it belongs to what was, to our former selves.

Paul lists these unwanted relics in Ephesians 4: slander we may use to harm another, the bitterness we justify and then harbor, the anger revealed in our responses to others. Paul encourages us to exchange the old for the new, and to be kind, tenderhearted, and forgive one another. Like taking off an old sweater that is no longer attractive, and putting on a new one. How long does that take? Not very long, although it is a process we must continually repeat. We remove who we used to be and live according to our new identity, our new life in Christ.

Everywhere the apostle Paul traveled, he shared the same encouragement, because all people need to hear it. We are all affected by the same dilemma. He reminds his young church in Colossae they are God's chosen ones and should behave according to their new identity. "Put on then, as God's chosen ones, holy and beloved, compassionate hearts, kindness, humility, meekness, and patience, bearing with one another and, if one has a complaint against another, forgiving each other; as the Lord has forgiven you, so you also must forgive" (Colossians 3:12-13).

Let's return the relics of the past to where they belong and live according to our new life in Christ.

Dear Lord, when unwanted relics of my past resurface, help me to put them away for good and live according to my new identity in you. Amen.

No other religion, no other, promises new bodies, hearts, and minds. Only in the gospel of Christ do hurting people find such incredible hope.

-Joni Eareckson Tada

26
Solitude

But when you pray, go into your room and shut
the door and pray to your Father
(Matthew 6:6).

A shady porch, a rocking chair, and a gentle breeze. An invitation to quiet time. Throughout history, men and women of faith have sought out time alone with God after realizing they can't multi-task a relationship with Him. They seek solitude, being alone, so they can meditate and pray. Even for the mature and those who know the importance of this practice, it is often elusive.

Phones and multiple forms of connectivity provide constant distractions. We find sitting alone in a room surrounded by the quiet to be difficult. A stream of distractions hits us like water from a multihead shower. We get caught up in a busy cycle and feel guilty if we sit down for even a few moments. We should be doing the dishes, writing that letter, cleaning the closet, pulling those pesky weeds, and responding to emails and scrolling through social media.

Depending on the source, the Bible contains more than six hundred references to prayer. If God said this much about prayer, He must know how much we need it. In Colossians 4:2, the apostle Paul instructs his spiritual children to "continue steadfastly in prayer, being watchful in it with thanksgiving." We often go about our business without seeking God's wisdom, thinking we're doing just fine in our own power.

Jesus prioritized time with His Father in prayer. He could have used that time to heal the sick, feed the poor, and teach. But even as people clamored for His attention, Jesus might withdraw to a quiet place to pray to His Father. He taught His disciples to do the same. In Matthew 6:6, Jesus told His followers, "But when you pray, go into your room and shut the door and pray to your Father who is in secret."

We all want to pray effectively. But when we have the King's ear, do we know what to say to Him? Though we may desire to approach our Father, knowing how to begin can be difficult. In Luke 11:1-4, the disciples observed Jesus praying, and one made a request: "Lord, teach us to pray, as John taught his disciples." Jesus modeled for them how to pray by sharing a portion of the Lord's Prayer. In this simple prayer, Jesus gave His disciples five clear steps: praise God's name, focus on His kingdom, ask for daily provision, embrace forgiveness, and pray for protection.

Most Christians would like their prayer life to be *more*. Almost every physical change we desire requires a plan for daily exercise. Daily exercise and exertion builds strength, and this is true of prayer. Which one of us hasn't been encouraged by spending time with a friend to listen, share, and renew our connection? The relationship is refreshed and satisfied. The same happens with prayer.

Sit. Rest. Be alone.

Listen. Pray. Reflect.

Be refreshed and filled by your time with God.

Lord, as your disciples asked, teach me how to pray. Remind me of my need to seek solitude from the busyness of life and to be with you alone. Amen.

27
Glass

I am with you and will watch over you wherever you go (Genesis 28:15 NIV).

The salvaged doors from a 1920s church stood upright against the wall of the old barn. Stan removed one at a time and carefully set each aside, revealing the door behind it.

"Look at this one," he said.

While we wiped away layers of dust, we counted ten glass panels, all with antique textured glass except one. On the second row down from the top, we discovered one clear pane. Eventually, we uncovered four glass panel doors. Each one had nine textured glass pieces and one clear pane in the exact same location. In an aha moment, we realized these were the Sunday school doors. The clear pane allowed parents to check on children in their classrooms.

Through a little research, we discovered the floral textured glass was called Florex, a Victorian fancy pattern patented in 1895. After some major cleaning and minor repairs, we used three of the four doors in the downstairs hallway of the farmhouse. Now, when we grasp the handle to enter the rooms, we are reminded of God's promise to watch over us wherever we go.

King David was comforted by this same understanding, and he often wrote about it. Psalm 73 is a beautiful depiction of an earthly king who is fully aware of his sin and limitations. Though he declares himself foolish in his own heart (verses 21-22), David rejoices in Psalm 73:23, "Nevertheless, I am continually with you." Regardless of his sin, he belongs to God one hundred percent of every day and every night. Continually means constantly and without interruption. We experience no break in our relationship with our heavenly Father. This is a great comfort to the believer.

The Lord holds us in His hand, guides us with His counsel, and will one day receive us to glory (Psalm 73:23-24). We are always on His heart. The Lord does not merely check in on us occasionally to make sure we are okay. He guards our going out and our coming in every second, every minute of our day. Because we are His children, we are the natural objects of His interest, and He welcomes us to draw near. David declares how good it is to be near God. In Psalm 73:28, he says, "But for me it is good to be near God; I have made the Lord God my refuge, that I may tell of all your works."

How comforting to know we are never outside of God's tender care. No barriers exist between us and our Heavenly Father.

Lord, help me remember I am continually on your mind and heart, and safe in your hand. Allow me to feel your presence and seek you as a refuge. Thank you for watching over me wherever I go. Amen.

28
Jazz

And I will ask the Father, and he will give you
another Helper, to be with you forever
(John 14:16).

If you have never seen a 1,000-pound Labrador retriever, you have not met Jazz. We know Jazz is a horse, not a dog, but he doesn't see it that way. A sleek chestnut Missouri Fox Trotter, Jazz follows Stan around like a giant puppy. If Stan needs to work on a fence inside the corral, Jazz is in his space, acting more curious than affectionate. He wants to sniff the tools and supplies. To get a better view, Jazz will shove his head between Stan and the project he is working on. Every time.

Jazz is eager to help. Unfortunately, without opposable thumbs and the knowledge of how to use tools, a horse is not very helpful when it comes to repairs on a farm. Even a well-intentioned horse. Jazz ends up simply getting in the way. Stan laughs about it and says, "I can do that repair in thirty minutes without Jazz or sixty minutes with him." When Stan has limited time to complete a project, Jazz is often sequestered in a different section of the corral. Stan needs a helper, but Jazz is not the right one.

Thankfully, we have a Helper who is both well-intentioned and able. When Jesus told His disciples at the Last Supper (John 14) that He was soon to leave them, they felt abandoned and fearful of the future. How could they go on without their powerful leader, the One whom even the wind and the seas obeyed? Jesus assured them even though He would no longer be with them, He would send another. This Spirit would indwell them, advocate for their good, and never leave them alone. The perfect Helper.

Perhaps the most encouraging way for us to understand the Holy Spirit is to realize He possesses every attribute of Jesus, yet without a physical body. Think how important this understanding was to the disciples when Jesus explained He would no longer be physically with them. Now, imagine Jesus helping us as He promised, being with us in all His ability and wisdom. "When the Spirit of truth comes, he will guide you into all the truth, for he will not speak on his own authority, but whatever he hears he will speak, and he will declare to you the things that are to come" (John 16:13).

The intention of the Holy Spirit is to bring us everything we lack. He will remind us of all Jesus said, a continuous loop of wisdom and encouragement. With the indwelling of the Spirit, evangelism is expanded. Jesus assures the disciples they will do greater works than He did (John 14:12). They were not to worry, because the Spirit would bring to their minds important things to share (John 14:25-26).

Jesus knew just what we needed. Our dependence on the Helper will lead to an obedient life, full of God's blessings.

> *Lord, thank you for being with me as I study your word. I pray your Spirit will guide me into greater understanding of the Christian life. Amen.*

29
Story

> As you received Christ Jesus the Lord, so walk in him, rooted and built up in him and established in the faith, just as you were taught, abounding in thanksgiving
> (Colossians 2:6-7).

The first time our oldest son, David, walked out of the house to get into a car and drive off on his own, I stopped him at the door and said, "Remember who you are."

I wanted David to remember that he was a young man on the brink of adulthood, a teen who had professed his faith in Jesus several years earlier, and a member of the Schuermann family. Understanding our place in our physical family and our spiritual family, matters. We prayed he would walk accordingly.

During the farmhouse construction, Stan and I committed to displaying family history wherever we could. We wanted our sons and grandchildren to have a bigger picture of where they came from. From vintage family photographs and history on the walls to dozens of photo albums, the grandchildren have opportunities to find out about past family members.

Knowing their stories gives them a greater sense of belonging, identity, purpose, and responsibility. When did our ancestors come to America? Were they farmers, business owners, or missionaries? What challenges did they overcome? We rejoice in their victories and learn from their mistakes. The more we know about our own family history, the more we feel part of something bigger than ourselves.

Just as our family history began long before we were born, our spiritual story began even farther back. The Bible tells us God chose us before the earth existed, long before our world came to be. "He chose us in him before the foundation of the world" (Ephesians 1:4). From all eternity, God knew us and said, "This one is mine."

The Bible is the telling of the Greatest Story—the story of how the Creator God formed the world and everything in it. We learn how God stopped at nothing to redeem fallen man and bring him back into fellowship. Now part of something much bigger than ourselves, we who are in Christ have a new story to tell of our redemption and the sweet relationship we enjoy with Him.

We can be thankful for the mercies God showed to us through our earthly family, in the good and the not so good. But we also have a new family of believers, a new future, and a new hope. Our identity flows from knowing our earthly story *and* our spiritual story.

By having a place in God's grand plan, we enjoy the privilege of calling God our Father. He sees us as His children. Throughout the Scripture, He reminds us of our relationship over and over again. "But to all who did receive him, who believed in his name, he gave the right to become children of God" (John 1:12).

How wonderful to know our destiny. Remember who you are.

Heavenly Father, you knew me before the world existed and named me as one of your children. Thank you for including me in your greatest story and giving me the privilege of calling you Father. Amen.

30
Pantry

> Oh, how abundant is your goodness, which
> you have stored up for those who fear you and
> worked for those who take refuge in you
> (Psalm 31:19).

When our boys were young, a trip to visit Stan's grandmother at her rural farmhouse meant a sweet Grandma hug and ... pull-a-parts. Those yummy little rolls coated in butter, cinnamon and sugar were always available, always accessible. Every time we visited, she almost magically produced them from various hiding places in her small kitchen.

My version of pull-a-parts is my GFFC recipe—Grammy's Famous Frozen Cookies. Always available in the pantry freezer, always accessible. The ornate Victorian pantry door with its antique butterfly hinges usually stands open. To us, the open door indicates someone recently accessed the goodies inside and invites the next person to do the same.

Lined with wooden tables and shelves, the eight foot by thirteen foot room contains foods to sustain the grandchildren, as well as treats, those little extras to delight the palate. The pantry doubles as a shelter, a refuge from an occasional Oklahoma storm. Though the adults pray we do not experience severe weather, the children look forward to sheltering in the pantry with all the goodies.

Unfortunately, the storehouse of food and supplies in the pantry can be depleted and requires frequent management, sorting, and evaluating. Outdated foods need to be discarded and staples restocked. Not so with God's storehouses.

No matter how famished we are, the supply of goodness will never run out in God's pantry. He filled the storehouses with good things before we were born, knowing exactly what we would need. What will we find there? The apostle Paul says God will show us the "immeasurable riches of his grace in kindness toward us in Christ Jesus" (Ephesians 2:7). Grace without measure. Never-ending goodness. Infinite kindness. The treasures are not gold or expensive goods, but spiritual blessings in abundance.

In Psalm 31:20-22, David declares God is a refuge and a shelter to all who trust in Him. Do you need encouragement? God hears when you seek Him and will affirm His love for you. He fills the storehouse to the brim with you in mind and extends an invitation to come and take freely of His treasures. Just as Grandma was pleased when we visited and enjoyed her tasty treats, our Father is well-pleased when we enter His storehouse and access the heavenly food He has provided through Jesus Christ.

Yes, it is all here for you. The pantry door stands permanently open.

Dear Heavenly Father, you care for me in ways I do not even realize. I praise you for storing up your riches and delights for me to enjoy. Grant me understanding to not take this privilege for granted but to be grateful. Amen.

31
Stars

> Lift up your eyes on high and see: who created these? He who brings out their host by number, calling them all by name; by the greatness of his might and because he is strong in power, not one is missing
> (Isaiah 40:26).

As much as the family loves the daylight hours at The Farm, excitement grows when night falls over the land. Especially on a clear night. When it is dark enough, we turn off the outside lights on the farmhouse and begin the night hike. Young and old, fast and slow, head up to the top of the dam with headlamps and flashlights. When all are gathered on the dam, we turn off the lights and behold the magnificent night sky.

The adults point out well-known constellations, and the children, squinting into the sky, attempt to discover new ones. We always mark the familiar: the North Star, Venus, Orion's Belt, the Big and Little Dippers.

With unaided vision, we can see thousands of twinkling lights. Beyond those are tens of billions more.

Astronomers estimate the galaxy we live in, the Milky Way, has about one hundred billion stars. Scientists estimate God's universe contains two trillion more galaxies beyond ours, each with billions of stars. Our great God determined the number and knows each star by name. The planets and stars are not braced into place or suspended by ropes. Each one occupies the space God intended.

In Psalm 8:3-4, the psalmist says, "When I look at your heavens, the work of your fingers, the moon and the stars, which you have set in place, what is man, that you are mindful of him, and the son of man that you care for him?" When we stand under the glory of a night sky filled with stars and planets and moons, we might ask the same question.

Do we think the God of the universe who knows the names of billions upon billions of stars would forget our name? The psalmist assures us God is mindful of His people. He thinks about us and cares for our well-being.

If God being mindful of man wasn't enough, Psalm 8:4-8 tells us we were given a place a little lower than the heavenly beings and crowned with glory and honor. God has given us dominion and stewardship over the earth and put all things under our feet. He redeemed us for this and created the world with man in mind.

The next time we step outside at night to a symphony of twinkling stars, we can be assured. We are precious in God's sight, created for a purpose. He delights in us, and He knows our name. Matthew 10:30 says God knows the number of hairs on our heads.

We are in no danger of being forgotten by Him.

Lord, I can't begin to comprehend your power and your glory. I am humbled and grateful that you see me, and you know my name. Thank you for keeping me forever in your care. Amen.

32
Repurposed

Many are the plans in the mind of a man, but it is the purpose of the Lord that will stand (Proverbs 19:21).

Occasionally during the construction phase of the farmhouse, a friend called to offer building materials they did not need. Our typical response was "We'll take it!" even if we had no idea how to utilize the items.

The day a friend offered new hickory flooring was no exception. After an improper installation in a new home, the boards were pried up and discarded into a pile, destined only to make a great-smelling campfire. Until that time, the materials were used as intended, but we had a different plan. We found a place where they would be redeemed and made perfect. Not just useful again, but perfect. After removing hundreds of embedded nails, we used the hickory flooring to create feature walls in the mudroom and mud bath. Here, their gifts and beauty were displayed and appreciated.

We humans like to plan out our lives, often in great detail. It is in our nature to plan for the future. And we should. Yet every plan should be made with God's wisdom and will. Our purposes often change, shifting with the day, the mood, or the experience. God sees our future differently than we do. We may see ourselves doing *this*, but God has plans for us to do *that*. His plan is perfect.

God is the master builder and when we place ourselves in His hands, we will flourish within His design. In the process of sanctifying us for His purpose and glory, God is at work removing all those things in our lives that limit our effectiveness. The process may be painful, as was the work to remove the nails, but it's always necessary.

We may feel we're living in a splintery pile and are no longer useful for the Master Builder's work. But God rescues us from an unfruitful life. He redeems us, transforms us, and makes us perfect for His glory.

In Jeremiah 29:11 (NIV), the message is clear: "For I know the plans I have for you … plans to prosper you and not to harm you, plans to give you hope and a future." God wants men and women to grow up (Ephesians 4:14-15). He wants us to increase in wisdom and knowledge (Ephesians 1:17-19) and to be ambassadors in His great commission work (2 Corinthians 5:20).

Don't be surprised when God redirects you. He is moving history toward the fulfillment of His great story, the redemption of all things in Christ. Our plans may shift and fluctuate, but God's counsel is perfect. The surest way to safety is to seek and follow the Lord's leading.

> *Dear Lord, thank you for revealing the plans you have for my life. Fulfill your purpose for me and give me the wisdom and strength to walk accordingly. Amen.*

33
Treasures

> Do not lay up for yourselves treasures on earth ... but lay up for yourselves treasures in heaven, where neither moth nor rust destroys and where thieves do not break in and steal. For where your treasure is, there your heart will be also (Matthew 6:19-21).

Many years ago, my dad told me about a wall hanging in his grandmother's farmhouse kitchen. It read:

A cheerful kitchen is our boast ...

Good hot tea and piping toast.

One year for Christmas, I asked a friend to make him a framed embroidery of this verse that now also hangs in our farmhouse kitchen. A treasure that brings delightful memories of my dad to mind.

Stan's great-grandmother was appointed postmaster in Kentucky in January 1904, and received a large certificate, signed, and sealed with the seal of the State of Kentucky. It now hangs in the Reading Room in an antique frame. In the same room, my grandmother's deaconess license from the British Columbia Methodist Church dated May 1916, graces the wall.

Old photographs of ancestors, hand-drawn family trees, and my mother's china teacups on delicate Victorian shelves, decorate various rooms and give us a sense of history. We consider them special treasures for our children and future generations. Beyond these emotional keepsakes, we appreciate having a home, vehicles to use, and this beloved farmhouse and surrounding land.

In the Sermon on the Mount, Jesus speaks of other treasures far more important than any on earth. He warns us to not hold material things too tightly and not make the focus of our life gathering possessions. Though we may love these items, all are vulnerable to decay, rust, and theft. Ultimately, they are not dependable and will not fulfill us. Our worldly treasures will not go with us when we go to heaven. We will keep only the good things we have done for the kingdom.

Besides reminding us to not stockpile earthly treasures, Jesus gives us many ways to store up treasures in heaven. When speaking to the multitudes in the Sermon on the Mount, Jesus mentions the meek and humble, and those seeking a life of righteousness. These will be satisfied, He said. Jesus referred to the merciful, the pure in heart, and the peacemakers. Those who extend forgiveness, give hope, and encourage others experiencing pain and affliction. These individuals will receive mercy and will be called the sons of God.

Spend some time with Jesus's sermon in Matthew 5-7. Make a list of all the ways we are to seek what is most important while living here on earth. Of course, we work to provide for our families and enjoy the fruit of our labor. We enjoy family treasures, but Jesus is clear we should seek to store up treasures for eternity and God's glory. A devout life brings us great spiritual riches.

In Matthew 7:24, Jesus sums up His sermon by telling us how to be wise. "Everyone then who hears these words of mine and does them will be like a wise man who built his house on the rock."

Dear Lord, give me a heart for your people and reveal my error when I start to lay up treasures on earth. I want my focus to be on your purposes and furthering your kingdom. Amen.

34
Laundry

Whatever you do, work heartily, as for the Lord and not for men, knowing that from the Lord you will receive the inheritance as your reward. You are serving the Lord Christ (Colossians 3:23-24).

Weaving my way through crowded downtown streets in Oklahoma City, I finally found the address and slowed my car to evaluate the used plumbing parts store. Sketchy. In my hunt for old things, I had entered many questionable places, but this was possibly the sketchiest store yet. And I was by myself.

I turned at the next corner and drove around the block, quickly parked, and left Stan a voicemail. "Just want someone to know where I am in case you don't hear back from me." I gave him the address and said, "I'm going in."

To say the experience was creepy is an understatement. Following a shirtless man in baggy cut-offs, I wandered through room after room of used toilets, sinks, hot water tanks, and tubs, in the dim light of the window-less building. Thirty minutes later, I emerged into the sunlight, safe and sound, with a 1922 Standard porcelain laundry sink. On the way home, I wondered how many people had stood at the sink and washed their clothes or scrubbed their hands after working in the fields.

One of our family's favorite sayings is, "A working boy is a happy boy." Our sons heard this many times as they were growing up, and we hear it repeated now by everyone from our grown boys to the youngest grandchild. "A working girl is a happy girl" works just as well.

Often, when the grandkids are doing chores, we ask, "Are you happy?" They reply, "I am *so* happy." This idea is not original to us, as the Bible has much to say about the importance of working with the right attitude.

The work we do today is rooted in God's design for the world. After God created Adam and Eve, He gave them specific tasks—to work in the Garden of Eden and maintain it (Genesis 2:15). He gave them the intellectual work of naming the animals and the cultural work of managing a family. God's desire was to work alongside man to preserve order in His creation.

When Jesus came to earth, He came to work and execute His Father's plan. In John 5, the apostle tells the story of Jesus healing a man by a pool in Bethesda on the Sabbath. When the Jews questioned Him on this, Jesus said, "My Father is working until now, and I am working" (John 5:17).

Though we are often frustrated with the work before us, sometimes feeling we are ill-equipped for the task, God can turn our limits into blessings. "Working as for the Lord" means honoring Him by working diligently and with the right attitude.

Reflect on how God blesses others by your commitment to caring for your home and your community. Maybe try singing a hymn the next time you tackle a mountain of laundry. And be thankful you aren't scrubbing those clothes on a scrub board in a 1922 laundry sink.

Ecclesiastes 3:22 (NIV) says, "There is nothing better for a person than to enjoy their work, because that is their lot."

Dear Father, bless the work of my hands and enable my efforts to bless others for your glory. When I grumble, bring to my mind how you are still working to gather a people for yourself. I pray my diligence will bring encouragement to others and further your kingdom. Amen.

35
Campfire

> The tested genuineness of your faith—more precious than gold that perishes though it is tested by fire—may be found to result in praise and glory and honor at the revelation of Jesus Christ (1 Peter 1:7).

Autumn at The Farm gets us all thinking about campfires. After the sun sets and we can no longer play kickball on the front lawn, we put on flannel shirts and gather a basket of hot dogs, buns, and condiments. Another basket is filled with the ingredients for s'mores, the campfire treat that delights everyone.

Anticipating a gathering at the campsite, someone builds the fire ahead of time. The flames finally subside, and the coals glow red, perfect for roasting hot dogs and marshmallows. The coals at the center of the fire pulse as if alive. Gazing into the coals, into the red glow, we find ourselves mesmerized by the intensity of the heat and the vibrant colors.

On a farm, many implements are strengthened through a fiery process called heat treating. The iron object is first subjected to a special fire with intense heat. It is then taken out of the fire and placed into a bath where the iron is cooled.

I can just hear the metal saying, "Ah, that's better." The result is metal with an increased capacity to withstand future stress. If it only experiences the fire, it will be weakened. But in combination with being immersed in cold water, the metal becomes stronger.

No person welcomes affliction. But as residents of this physical world, we regularly experience trials and tribulations. As much as affliction may hurt, it is not designed to destroy us, but rather to strengthen us, much as the extreme heat followed by a cool bath creates greater toughness in the iron. When we suffer, we might ask, "What are you doing, Lord?"

When we are in the middle of a trial, a lost job, a broken relationship, an unwelcome medical diagnosis, we may feel like we've been thrown into the campfire. But God tells us in 1 Peter 1:7 that our faith, though tested by fire, will bring glory and honor to our Lord.

The faith that triumphs in adversity is the most precious faith. Had we not experienced the affliction, we would not have known our own weakness, nor would we have seen the power of God quench the fire. The heat from a fiery trial is quenched by truth in the Word of God. Faith grows most when we experience opposition, and the result is a strengthening for the next time affliction comes. James 1:2-4 tells us testing results in steadfastness. For the Christian, suffering produces endurance, character, and hope, as we experience God's love pouring into our hearts through the Holy Spirit (Romans 5:3-5).

When you feel the weight of affliction, ask God to increase your faith and make you steadfast. Let His grace envelop you and strengthen your faith, so you can say with the psalmist in Psalm 107:8, "Let them thank the Lord for his steadfast love, for his wondrous works to the children of man!"

Dear Jesus, calm my spirit and increase my faith. Make me steadfast. You know my suffering and you have a plan to bring me the peace only you can give. Amen.

36
Image

If you had known me, you would have known my Father also. From now on you do know him and have seen him (John 14:7).

We are often blessed at The Farm with spectacular sunsets over the pond, especially in the fall and winter. During those seasons, the setting sun is positioned directly over the center of the pond where it narrows and flows to the west. When the water is still and the clouds are just right, the sight can be truly glorious. Sometimes the yellows and reds and oranges are king. Sometimes the blues reign. The reflection in the water is a perfect representation of the sky above, and any observer can hardly tell the real from the reflection.

We enlarged a few sunset photographs and framed the sixteen by twenty prints for the upstairs game room. Stan mounted one in a vintage frame and attached the cord to hang it from the picture rail with a copper hook. He even checked to make sure the image was right side up. Only later did we find out it wasn't.

A friend was there helping us for the afternoon and offered to go upstairs and hang the sunset picture. She took a while, and eventually returned carrying the frame. "I think this is upside down," she said.

We studied the print. Though the clouds on the water exactly matched the clouds in the sky, we oriented the image according to the tree line on the shore. The reflection was so perfect, Stan had unknowingly attached the cord to hang the picture upside down.

Jesus said if you know me, you know my Father. To know one is to know the other. Jesus is the perfect representation of His Father, the God above. Genesis 1:27 tells us God created men and women in His own image. We were made in the perfect image of Christ, the perfect obedient man. When Adam and Eve's disobedience marred this relationship, the image didn't go away. It was simply ruined because of sin. To save us all, Jesus came to earth, taking on the form of a man.

When we believe Jesus Christ is the Son of God, we gain all He recovered for us. We are no longer condemned by the sin that caused the problem in the first place. Though sin still dwells with us and mars the perfect image here, God's Spirit is at work in believers to change us. The Bible tells us to be like Christ in all we do, living the same way Jesus lived (1 John 2:6). We reflect the Father just as Jesus reflected the Father.

The Bible tells us God sees His Son in us. To God, we reflect Jesus (Romans 8:29). In this life, we may sometimes feel we are a poor representation of Jesus and the one we call Father. The more we spend time with another person, we learn what pleases them, what they enjoy. During this process, we become more united with them. You don't have to wait for heaven to know God.

Let the words of Jesus dwell richly within you and reflect the image of your Savior to others.

Lord, thank you for creating me in your image and for restoring me in Jesus. May I never forget the incredible gift of mercy I have been given. Amen.

37
Roots

> He is like a tree planted by water, that sends out
> its roots by the stream, and does not fear when
> heat comes, for its leaves remain green, and is
> not anxious in the year of drought, for it does
> not cease to bear fruit (Jeremiah 17:8).

A walk on the one hundred fifty-five acres of land reveals the blessing of thousands of trees. With mighty oaks and pecan trees, hackberry, elm, and many others, our farm is a unique piece of farmland. Woods, rolling hills, ravines, and small creeks weave through the acreage.

Our biggest trees are the ones that grow near water, along the creeks and ravines. Their roots go down deep seeking the underground source, and their branches reach high toward the sun. Smaller trees dot the hillsides where they are more vulnerable to the elements and less able to reach water. They are shaded from the sunlight they need and are often spindly and weak.

Several years ago, a great ice storm ravaged thousands of acres across the state. Limbs littered the ground across the farm, broken off and tossed at the base of the trees. In some cases, the entire tree toppled over in a mass of snapped branches. Many trees withered and died.

Some downed trees remained alive even though severely wounded and bowed down to the ground. Laid low amid their own mangled branches, their roots remained attached, reaching deep into the earth, and holding tight. They were not about to give up even if laying on the ground, and continued to produce new green leaves and blooms of flowers. They had what we might call staying power.

Troubles come to the unbeliever and believer alike. Just by the mere fact that we wake up in the world, we have frustration, anxiety, concerns, and disappointments. When the storm rages and when the heat threatens to overtake us, do we draw on the source of life? Just as the thirsty tree sends its roots down deep, we need to reach for the nourishment provided by our God and Savior.

The world gives us bad news. Jesus gives us good news. He is the rescuer. Jesus beckons us, "Come to me" (Matthew 11:28). He will replace life's difficulties with peace and joy. This is the only way we will be able to endure hardship and tribulation. Blessed are they who have made God their hope and sustaining source.

Psalm 1:3 tells us if we are like trees planted by streams of water, reaching deep to the secret source of life, our leaves will not wither. Our roots will go down to find strength, and we will not be destroyed by hardship. Colossians 2:7 (TLB) reminds us, "Let your roots grow down into him and draw up nourishment from him. See that you go on growing in the Lord, and become strong and vigorous in the truth you were taught."

Dear Lord, teach me how to reach deep to draw on your sustaining power. Thank you for holding me up in times of hardship and drought and for making me stronger through affliction. Amen.

38
Reflection

My grace is sufficient for you, for my power is made perfect in weakness
(2 Corinthians 12:9).

Life this side of heaven will never be perfect, though the day Stan rowed me around the farm pond seemed nearly so. Trees along the shore and the clouds above them reflected into the still water. The only difference between the real thing and the reflection were tiny ripples.

The oarlocks squeaked slightly when Stan rowed, not enough to irritate, but he did mention a dose of WD40 when we returned to the dock. While water bugs danced on the water's surface, the birds called overhead as they circled the pond. I did note some of the larger birds were vultures, but Stan said, "Don't worry, just look alive."

Occasionally a fish jumped several yards away and I'd shout, "Row over there." Stan spoiled me by doing as I asked. Every now and then, I peeked into the old ice chest to count the fish, thinking about the fish tacos we would have for dinner that night.

Across the pond, even the cormorants were in good form. They stood like statues on exposed tree stumps, lifting their wings high, attempting to dry their feathers. Although they lack the adornments and graces of other water birds, the cormorants are who they were designed to be. If they indulged in comparison to validate their perfection, they would likely be discouraged. However, by God's design, they are beautiful.

Thankfully, God never asked *me* to be a perfect person, a perfect wife, a perfect mom, a perfect daughter, or daughter-in-law. He doesn't even expect me to never make a mistake as a grandmother or mother-in-law. And, for that, I am very thankful. Life is not perfectible. We have challenges, trials, discouragements, disappointments, pain, sorrow, regrets, guilt … yikes.

When Jesus says, "Be perfect, therefore, as your heavenly Father is perfect" in Matthew 5:48 (NIV), He is urging His followers toward eventual "completeness" or maturity when He returns for us. For now, God is growing us up toward this maturity through the process of sanctification. His plan is to use our weaknesses and the not-so-perfect events in our lives to bring us closer to Him. And to help us move toward completeness.

Imperfection is one of the few things all humans still have in common. When we're conscious of our weakness and look to God for help, forgiveness is ours because we have an advocate in Jesus. 1 John 2:1 tells us, "If anyone does sin, we have an advocate with the Father, Jesus Christ the righteous." His grace is sufficient.

In our humility, God gives us the perfection of justification in Jesus. Let's leave ourselves in His hands. We will not be perfect this side of heaven, but we can be at peace, and we can grow. "Since we have been justified by faith, we have peace with God through our Lord Jesus Christ" (Romans 5:1).

It is all in God's perfect plan.

Dear Lord, when I attempt to rely on my own wisdom, remind me to rely on you. Show me my weaknesses and lead me to your throne. Guide me on the journey toward completeness in Jesus. Amen.

39
Contentment

> I have learned in whatever situation I am to be content (Philippians 4:11).

Stacks of books sit on the coffee table in our living room. Books about identifying Oklahoma songbirds, knowing your ducks and geese, and finding constellations on a starlit night, among others. A large burgundy book, *The History of Grant County Families*,[6] from The Grant County Historical Society is usually within reach.

Grant County is north of The Farm and where my father-in-law spent his childhood. Accounts of families who built homes and cultivated the untamed land fill this book; it even includes a story about the Schuermann traveling band. Of all the tales of strength and resilience, my favorite is about a young bride named Tillie.

"Almost there, Tillie." George called back to the young woman in the wagon.

His bride squinted her eyes to see ahead in the bright sun. Despite the jostling of the wagon on the rough terrain, she was able to make out a small frame house sitting unceremoniously in the middle of a pasture. A *claim house*, as it was called. No trees. Just tall grass and weeds lapping the siding in the Oklahoma wind. Far from Kansas City.

George, excited about bringing his new wife to the house on his newly-acquired land, ushered Tillie into the tiny living space. He left her for a moment and retrieved a wooden rocking chair from the wagon. While George unhitched and fed the team, Tillie sat in the chair and surveyed her new home. Clapboard walls, dusty wood floors, no running water. George returned inside to find her sobbing over her new primitive home.

Happily, the story doesn't end with Tillie crying in her tiny house. The account goes on to tell us the very next morning, she woke up bright and early and began unpacking, hanging curtains, arranging the meager furnishings, and singing hymns. Tillie found and expressed her contentment in praise and song.

Through the years, Tillie was loved by her neighbors who delighted in her singing and called her their songbird. All because she made a choice to be content, to be grateful. Tillie was satisfied with her life, because she found what she was looking for in God.

When the apostle Paul said, "I have learned in whatever situation I am to be content," his plight was far worse than Tillie's. He was an elderly man, locked in a bleak dungeon in Nero's Rome. Historians believe he spent two years in prison there. Paul makes clear that contentment does not come naturally to us; it is a learned skill. No matter the trials he experienced and his great need, he had joy and contentment because he trusted God to provide for his true needs.

Contentment is a beautiful thing but doesn't naturally grow in us. It must be cultivated like the flowers in our gardens. In Psalm 73:25-26, the psalmist turns to the Lord with hope and anticipation. "Whom have I in heaven but you? And there is nothing on earth that I desire besides you. My flesh and my heart may fail, but God is the strength of my heart and my portion forever."

Dear Lord, the skill of contentment is not natural to me, but I want to learn how to cultivate it. Teach me how to experience great joy and contentment in you regardless of my circumstances. Amen.

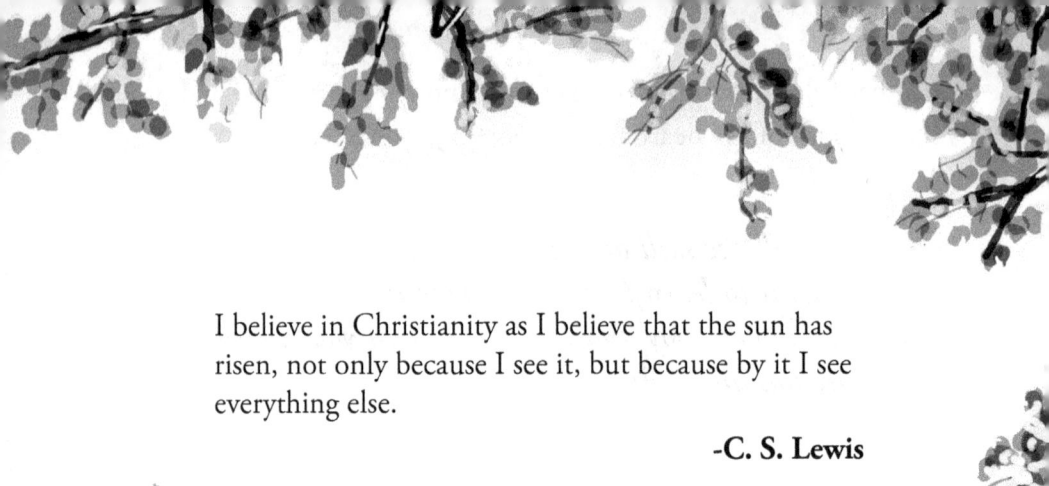

I believe in Christianity as I believe that the sun has risen, not only because I see it, but because by it I see everything else.

-C. S. Lewis

40
Morning

> And God saw that the light was good. And God
> separated the light from the darkness
> (Genesis 1:4).

Early mornings at the farm are my favorite, especially when darkness still envelops the land. In early dawn, streams of light reach like fingers across the darkness. They explode and overtake the night as light illuminates the ground, the trees, and the water. Sometimes slowly, often quickly, the darkness fades away and is no more. A new day, a fresh beginning, another opportunity to live life. And enjoy coffee.

When God said it was good to separate the day and night, He knew exactly what we needed. Even the blackest night gives way to morning. Creatures of the darkness flee the light, and the creatures of the day come alive. Birds begin their songs even before the light dawns, and their melodies grow to a crescendo as the sun peeks over the horizon. Racoons and possums that rooted around in the yard and on the back porch during the night retreat to their daytime dens and are nowhere to be seen.

According to Genesis, in the beginning, the earth was covered in darkness. God spoke, "Let there be light" (Genesis 1:3) and there was light. God divided light from darkness and made morning and evening. Light and darkness fade into each other, but they cannot work together. They are separate from one another and can't exist in the same space at the same time.

Physical light is from God. He fashioned us to dwell in it just as He made the creatures of the dark to flee the light. Light reveals the beauty of creation, as well as the imperfections of the world. The weeds in the lawn may not bother us during the night when we can't see them, but they practically leap into our view in the light of day.

At God's direction, we experience spiritual light when the Holy Spirit opens our eyes to recognize God in the person of Jesus Christ. We have a new ability to see. When our sin is revealed, we flee it and ask God to cleanse us.

Jesus said, "I am the light of the world. Whoever follows me will not walk in darkness, but will have the light of life" (John 8:12). Think about how your perspective changed when you came to know Jesus Christ. You began to see the world through the lens of the One who created it, as if you put on a new pair of glasses.

Jesus is the radiance of the glory of God (Hebrews 1:3). If you are in a dark place, know the Source of light is available. If you come to Him, you will begin to see clearly. When you see the first glimmer of spiritual light on the horizon, welcome it as your companion, a comforting blanket. Jesus will illuminate your soul and help you peer past the darkness.

It is here—in the light—that we have hope.

Heavenly Father, teach me how to walk in the light of your love and mercy. Let your light shine through me. Amen.

41
Walk

Take my yoke upon you, and learn from me, for I am gentle and lowly in heart, and you will find rest for your souls (Matthew 11:29).

We love many things about The Farm, including how we are so easily entertained here. A walk outdoors opens abundant opportunities for adventure, fun, and discovery. The short hike up to the dam reveals a bird's eye view of the farmhouse on one side and the pond on the other. Even a simple walk to the horse corral to give Jazz a couple of apples delights and satisfies.

Some walkers stay close to the farmhouse, but others venture far into the meadows and untamed woods using maps for guidance. Some use walking sticks. Others run, but all enjoy the freedom of being in the great wide open. Whether in shorts and T-shirts in the summer or bundled against the cold in winter, a hike is always a welcome event. Treasures such as animal bones and turtle shells often come back to the farmhouse with the hikers and pile up on the porch for further examination.

Instruction for the hikes usually includes a dose of caution. During the winter, the explorers can venture into the untamed parts of the land without concern. But between March and the first hard freeze in late fall, hikers are urged to stay on the paths.

Our guys regularly mow the walking paths to keep us safe. A manicured path allows us to see dangers, things that may harm us like poison ivy or even rattlesnakes.

When our grandchildren were younger, one or more of them would run out of steam and return to the farmhouse sitting on their dad's shoulders. The children needed the strength of another to carry them home.

In Matthew 11, Jesus spoke to a crowd, inviting them to walk with Him. He shared an illustration familiar to the listeners—the yoke, a harness used with oxen to make hauling a load easier. Often, an experienced animal was paired with one in training. Tethered together, the experienced animal set the pace, while the inexperienced animal leaned in for support. In verses 29-30, Jesus said, "Take my yoke upon you, and learn from me, for I am gentle and lowly in heart, and you will find rest for your souls. For my yoke is easy, and my burden is light." Jesus invites us to take His yoke.

When we become weary and discouraged in our own strength, Jesus assures us He is the strong one and invites us to walk with Him, learn from Him, and lean on Him for support. He assures us this walk will be safe for He has placed us on His shoulders. Remember, our security is not found in our strength but in His.

If we are weary, Jesus remains strong. If we lack faith, He remains faithful. The path of faith is easier than the path of unbelief because Jesus's yoke is easy, and His burden is light.

Lord, teach me how to walk with you. In your strength, I will progress in my faith, even through challenges. Show me how to make walking with you the visible theme of my life. Amen.

42
Ordinary

> Who among all these does not know that the
> hand of the Lord has done this? In his hand is
> the life of every living thing and the breath
> of all mankind (Job 12:9-10).

Ordinary things can be easily overlooked in our world today. When images of the latest, greatest, and flashiest grab our attention, the simple and the everyday can seem uninteresting.

But God, in His infinite wisdom, gave us all things to enjoy, and He pronounced what He created to be special. And He gave us our senses: sight, hearing, smell, taste, and the ability to touch and feel. He tells us to pay attention, because everything He has blessed us with on this earth should point us to Him. The animals and the plants are examples of God's wisdom in design. So are we.

During the day, we often take a break from the chores, grab a cool drink, and rock in the rocking chairs on the porch. Someone might easily break into singing "Oklahoma!" when birds soar overhead. "We sit alone and talk and watch a hawk makin' lazy circles in the sky."

Though we do see hawks and an occasional bald eagle, most of the big birds circling above us are vultures. I'm learning to enjoy them too. Catching the wind currents, they float in the sky like skillful hang gliders.

We will never forget the day we watched the fat, neon green caterpillar miraculously spin his chrysalis before our eyes. About two weeks later, a lovely, soft-green luna moth emerged and unfolded its wings. After fluttering for a few seconds on the ground, it took off into its new life.

Our eyes delight in a field of wildflowers. Individually they each have their own beauty. Together, they are a plush blanket of colors and textures, beckoning someone to lie down among them. Our ears find the whippoorwill's announcement of coming nightfall warm and comforting. We may smile at a box full of new puppies or kittens, as long as they belong to someone else.

When God created the Garden overflowing with all things for Adam and Eve to enjoy, they must have been amazed at the variety and uniqueness of each plant and animal. As time went on, they may have become accustomed to God's creations, deeming them more ordinary than special. If you've seen one long-wattled umbrellabird, you've seen them all, right?

If the natural world around you has become *nothing special*, begin anew to discover the wonder of everyday things and see the world through the lens of God's love for you. Examine a flower closely, the colors and textures. Inspect an insect or your cat's paws and claws. Sit and observe your children playing. Watch a cloud float across the sky. Ask God to show you what He wants you to see. Relish those ordinary moments and ordinary days when He speaks to you in a unique way.

Declare something to be special and make it a celebration. Promote everyday experiences because what we deem ordinary may be extraordinary, after all.

Dear Lord, open my eyes to what you will teach me each day. I want to embrace the beauty of your world and look for the extraordinary in every ordinary thing. Amen.

43
Washed

But you were washed, you were sanctified, you were justified in the name of the Lord Jesus Christ and by the Spirit of our God (1 Corinthians 6:11).

After the delivery truck left us with several boxes of gleaming white toilets, the plumber stared at me in disbelief. He held the house plans in his hand and shook the papers for extra effect. "Ma'am, do you know how many bathrooms you have in this house?"

I nodded. "Yes, sir, I know." Though some were half-baths, they still needed toilets and sinks. "And I'm off to find antique washstands." I grinned at him.

I became a regular at every antique mall within driving distance, hunting for old marble-topped washstands from the early 1900s. Stan built custom vanities for the two bunkrooms. The mudroom bath features a

1910 porcelain pedestal sink we found in a junk store. We wondered if a famous or even notorious person might have shaved in this old sink.

All of the sinks serve an important purpose as washing is a frequent exercise at The Farm. We are continually scrubbing away something unwanted, something we picked up from daily interaction with the outside world—chiggers, dirt, germs, grasshopper goo, and grime, to name just a few. The day several grandchildren relocated buckets of tadpoles from a muddy pond to a creek, we were thankful for soap and water.

God offers good news for humanity in need of being made clean. In 1 Corinthians 6:9-11, the apostle Paul lists people caught up in the sin of this world, saying the unrighteous will not inherit the kingdom of God. He then says, "And such were some of you." Paul describes the great work of God in Jesus Christ with three words: washed, sanctified, and justified.

When we accepted the work of Jesus Christ on the cross, we were washed clean by His sacrifice. No matter what we have done, what sin we engaged in, Jesus washed us clean when we went to Him in faith. Titus 3:5 says, "He saved us, not because of works done by us in righteousness, but according to his own mercy, by the washing of regeneration and renewal of the Holy Spirit."

When God saved us and made us clean, He sanctified us, setting us apart from the rest of the world. He does not take us out of our environment but sends us back into the world with the power and protection of the Holy Spirit and the Word (John 17:15-18).

Rejoice in the fact that when God looks at us, He sees Jesus. He declares us to be just, not because we're full of good deeds but because of what Jesus did on our behalf. No matter how much *stuff* we pick up from the outside world, Jesus will make us clean, sanctify us, and justify us in His name, if we only believe.

Dear Lord, thank you that you care for the minor matters in my life. In the midst of many demands, bring to my mind all you have done for me and how you have washed me clean. Grant me the strength to live honorably and keep my eyes on you. Amen.

44
Night

You make darkness, and it is night, when all the beasts of the forest creep about (Psalm 104:20).

When dusk approaches in the spring, we sit in the rocking chairs on the porch, our ears listening for the call of the whippoorwills. In our area, we know them as chuck-will's-widows. Stan's mother told us they arrive at the same time every year, and she was right. They rarely miss April 19 by more than a day and are usually perfectly on time. If we stay outside past sundown during the summer months, the fireflies light up the yard while the moon peeks from behind the trees on the hill.

While the moon rises and the stars begin to twinkle, we stay and watch a while, marveling at the beauty. When the bushes rustle with critters and the coyotes howl, the younger grandchildren shudder, and it's time to go inside for ice cream. Soon, the raccoons will rattle the gas grill on the back porch and the armadillos will come out of their hiding places to dig for grubs in the lawn.

By nature, humans are afraid of what we don't understand. A few years ago, a backyard campout ended with grandchildren piling back into the house with their blankets, pillows, stuffed animals, and flashlights. "We don't like hoots and howls."

Without understanding, we're fearful and feel vulnerable. Our preferred environment is light. We were not made to dwell in darkness.

Owls, coyotes, opossums, and raccoons own the night, as their eyes were made to see in the dark. Their domain is darkness. God created these animals' eyes with more rods than human eyes, giving them special abilities and enabling them to see and hunt for food with the tiniest bit of light. And He arranged the night and day so all the creatures of the world could live together. While most humans work during the day and rest at night, the nocturnal animals work at night and rest during the day. This is a beautiful picture of the order God created.

For the Christian, the concepts of light and darkness have spiritual meaning, and the Bible has much to say about them. In both the Old Testament and the New Testament, light is good, and darkness denotes a life without God. Though the light of Jesus shines brightly for all to see, men continue to love darkness. John 3:19 says, "The light has come into the world, and people loved the darkness rather than the light because their works were evil."

Here is the best news: we do not need to fear darkness. It will never overcome the light of Jesus Christ. In John 1:5, the apostle says, "The light shines in the darkness, and the darkness has not overcome it." The darkness will never win.

Jesus said, "I am the light of the world. Whoever follows me will not walk in darkness, but will have the light of life" (John 8:12).

Dear Jesus, your Word is my lamp. You illuminate my darkness. Thank you for bringing me into the light of your presence. Amen.

45
Hope

But this I call to mind, and therefore I have hope (Lamentations 3:21).

When Stan and I built the farmhouse, one of our intentions was to preserve family history for future generations. Most of us know interesting stories of our ancestors and desire to pass them on to our kids and grands. If a contest were held among my friends, my ancestors' story might win a prize.

My mother's parents, Irus and Sara Purkeypile, served as teachers in a remote Eskimo village in the Territory of Alaska in the 1920s and '30s. In 1927, my mother was born into this life. She grew up skating on frozen rivers with Eskimo children, snowshoeing through several feet of snow, and managing her own dog sled team. A child's dream life.

My grandmother, Sara, loved flowers, sunshine, and summer, delights rarely enjoyed by someone living above the Arctic Circle. Sara was a woman of faith and trusted in God's promises. While she endured the darkness and cold of the winter months, she anticipated the time when the sunless days and bitter temperatures would give way to light and warmth.

In late April and May each year, Sara watched for the first signs of new life on the tundra, seedlings pushing their way through the melting snow and ice. When she saw them, she rejoiced with renewed hope the sun would shine again and for the good things to come. In a letter to a cousin in New Jersey, Sara wrote, "I look to the time when the water runs."

The return of the sun meant the ice on the frozen rivers and streams would break up and boats could run freely. Sara anticipated the future with gladness and confidence because she knew the God who supplied her needs again and again.

Often the greatest encouragement for our life yet to come can be found in looking at our past. In 1 Samuel 7, Samuel urged the house of Israel to return to the Lord with all their heart. Samuel declared, "Till now the Lord has helped us" (1 Samuel 7:12). He prayed the Lord might have mercy and save them from the hands of the Philistines. God did hear Samuel's pleadings and saved the people from destruction.

Samuel reminds the people they can trust their God who consistently provides, protects, and directs them, the God who has shown Himself to be trustworthy and faithful, year after year. Our hope is based on recalling how God has provided for us in the past. Our assurance comes from knowing the strength of the One whose promises we trust.

The God who caused the sun to shine and the water to run again in northern Alaska can be trusted. We have a secure hope we can count on. We all have stories of God's providential care and the many ways He has sustained us. He has proved himself faithful. Our families will gain confidence and hope as we tell them, "Till now the Lord has helped us."

Thank you, Lord, for your faithfulness and mercy. Help me recall the many ways you have provided for me in the past and give me hope for the future. Amen.

46
Rest

My presence will go with you, and I will give you rest (Exodus 33:14).

Nothing says stop and rest like a comfy chair on a breezy farmhouse porch in the country. The saying goes, "Relax, replenish, take a break, breathe. Take a load off your feet."

The two large white rockers on the back porch, and four on the front porch, often call out to us to stop and rest. They beckon us to a glass of iced tea, or maybe to read, ponder, meditate, and pray. Or visit with the person sitting next to us.

The back porch off the kitchen faces west, so it is the best choice in the mornings. Here we look out over the camp area with its lush, green canopy of trees, a shelter for the many songbirds.

In the afternoons, the front porch is protected from the sun by the house and is cooler than the back. Here we watch the hawks and an occasional eagle soar overhead. Even the vultures seem beautiful in flight. When children visit, the porch affords the best view of their frisbee, football, and kickball games. The perfect vantage point to rest and enjoy being together.

We tend to think resting means doing nothing. Busy moms dream of that illusive day with no commitments. Imagine no soccer games, no orthodontist appointments, no grocery shopping, and no store returns. Now that does sound restful. But if rest is restorative, there is some kind of restoring activity going on when we rest. Like when C-3PO in *Star Wars: A New Hope* requests permission to shut down, we sometimes need to give ourselves permission to recalibrate.

Themes of restoration, renewal, and rest are woven throughout the Bible. The foundation of biblical rest is laid out for us in Genesis 2:2 when God rested from His creative activity. The Hebrew word for rest used here is *sabbat*. "And on the seventh day God finished his work that he had done, and he rested (sabbat) on the seventh day from all his work that he had done" (Genesis 2:2).

In Mark 6:31, Jesus told His disciples, "Come away by yourselves to a desolate place and rest a while." They had been so busy in ministry to many, they had no time even to eat. Jesus recognized their need to pause, to be refreshed, and to abide in Him. He knew they needed to be restored in mind and body and gave them the gift of rest.

When responsibilities and stresses mount, take God's offer of restoration. Listen to His call to come away and rest awhile. Allow your body to unwind and recharge. The God of comfort promises to calm your heart and nourish your soul (Matthew 11:28).

Let Him wrap His arms around you, renewing you for another day, strengthening you with His power (Colossians 1:11).

Dear Lord Jesus, thank you for the gift of rest. Show me how to clear my cluttered mind and be refreshed and renewed by you. Amen.

Contentment is one of the flowers of heaven, and if we would have it, it must be cultivated; it will not grow in us by nature.

-Charles H. Spurgeon

47
Eagles

> They who wait for the LORD shall renew their strength; they shall mount up with wings like eagles; they shall run and not be weary; they shall walk and not faint (Isaiah 40:31).

We call it the day of the bald eagles, a day we will always remember. From the dam, we watched a pair of eagles soar over the pond. They flew in circles, one higher than the other, then they switched places, occasionally dipping down toward the water as if they spied a potential catch. After several minutes, they flew away through the trees, off to the next adventure.

Later after walking a few minutes on the trail, sound and movement above our heads startled us. We stood still, looking up at two eagles with six-foot wingspans soaring above us, barely clearing the treetops. Their wings *whooshed*, the best word we could come up with to describe the powerful sound. While we watched, the eagles whirled around each other in a beautiful dance in the sky. Then, as quickly as they came, they were gone. The power, the strength, and the freedom of these mighty birds left me with a twinge of envy.

Eagles hold a prominent place in Scripture as a symbol of strength and hope. In Isaiah 40, God speaks through His prophet to the Israelites to comfort them after they were displaced from their homes by the Babylonians. The people were discouraged and frightened, and God uses an analogy about eagles to lift them up from their despair. "They who wait for the Lord shall renew their strength; they shall mount up with wings like eagles; they shall run and not be weary; they shall walk and not faint" (Isaiah 40:31).

A little research on eagles reveals their tendency to wait for the right wind thermals. They may remain perched on a branch or cliff for days, awaiting the updraft they need to soar. Waiting is not necessarily passive. Isaiah urges the Israelites to wait with hope, trust, and confidence, anticipating what God might do in spite of their difficult circumstances. The Lord promises He will make those who wait on him stronger.

Who hasn't wished to be like a bird and fly high above our challenges on earth, to transcend those things that discourage or entangle us? Isaiah says if we wait for God, we will soar into the heavenly places. We will receive the endurance to walk the walk (Colossians 2:6) and the strength to run the race set before us without becoming exhausted (Hebrews 12:1).

Like the eagle who waits in the tree for the right time to fly, those who wait for God, our Deliverer, will receive power in weakness, strength to rise above the storms, and endurance for the journey.

Dear Heavenly Father, thank you for lifting me up when I fall, giving me renewed strength when I become weary, and enabling me to endure in times of difficulty. Teach me to wait on you. Amen.

48
Order

And God saw everything that he had made, and behold, it was very good (Genesis 1:31).

On any given day at the farmhouse, the grandchildren bring all sorts of findings to the front porch for further examination. Sometimes they show up with treasures they found in the woods, emptying their pockets of animal bones and teeth. We greet them with, "Let's see what you found this time." They dump the bones on the porch table to sort them. Rib bones here, leg bones there. Even as young children, they see order and purpose, and they want to know how things fit together. I'm not a fan of these things coming inside, although a turtle shell did take up residence on the kitchen counter for about a year.

Interesting conversations ensue over what kinds of animals the bones came from. Skulls show up from time to time. The children have identified skulls of a bobcat, raccoon, cow, coyote, deer, and even a turtle. Often we ask them, "What do you wonder about this?"

While the children examine the eye sockets, size and shape of the skull, and other features, they are full of questions. Even though they inquire, they know God created each animal with intent.

Sometimes we lay sprigs of grasses and wildflowers on the back porch or the dining table for comparison and identification. Using a book about Oklahoma prairie grasses, we flip through and look for the scientific name of each one, recording our findings in a journal. When the children tire of this activity, they run outside and catch grasshoppers.

Of course, the critters are all named immediately. Greenie, Hoppy, Jumpy. They all look alike to the adults, but somehow the grands can tell them apart. Or at least they pretend to.

God created a discoverable, orderly world that reflects His character. The Bible tells us God created the heavens and the earth out of disorder. "The earth was without form and void, and darkness was over the face of the deep" (Genesis 1:2). By the Spirit's power, God brought form and shape and order. From the placement of the galaxies to the position of the planets and stars, He put each in its proper place. He created day and night, the sun and the moon, separated water from dry land, and established the seasons. He made it all for His glory and for us to enjoy.

Unfortunately, because of Adam and Eve's rebellion and sin, we live in a world full of chaos and disorder. We see sickness where there was only health. We see separation, brokenness, and death, where there had been fellowship, wholeness, and life. God promises one day order will again triumph over chaos when righteousness triumphs over sin. He will remove the chaos of sin and restore the created order for those who trust in Jesus.

Even if our world seems disordered and confused, we can find rest and strength knowing God rules and overrules all things. The psalmist assures us, "Cast your burden on the Lord, and he will sustain you; he will never permit the righteous to be moved" (Psalm 55:22).

Let us draw daily on these comforting words and look to God the Creator to sustain us.

Dear Lord, you bring order to my life and to the world. Open my eyes to see intricate details of your creation. Touch me with a sense of awe and wonder. Amen.

49
Useful

The more you grow like this, the more productive and useful you will be in your knowledge of our Lord Jesus Christ (2 Peter 1:8 NLT).

One of the more curious items at The Farm is an old piece of farm equipment, nearly hidden in the trees by overgrown brush and thorny vines. In its day, this Allis Chalmers harvester combined the cutting and thrashing of wheat and other grain crops. We estimate it hasn't been used since the 1930s or '40s. At one time the tool was the most productive and best available. Now the machine sits idle, a faded painted sunburst on the grain bin the only reminder of a vibrant past life.

The harvester experienced years of neglect, changing seasons, and harsh elements. The trees and brush around it block most of the sunlight from getting through, but precipitation still finds a way to reach the metal. Curiously, nearly 100 years later, much of the sheet metal is untarnished, having a semblance of the life it had in the 1930s. This metal was galvanized for longevity. In contrast, the ungalvanized parts rusted. Sadly, the harvester had no ability to repair itself, and no one was there to protect it.

Many of us could barely contain our zeal and excitement—like love's first blush—when we first came to Christ. If we failed to regularly sustain the relationship with fresh wisdom, fresh zeal, and fresh desire, we may feel as if we are now on the sidelines growing rust. But God designed us to live a meaningful and purposeful life. With this design in mind, He teaches us how to thrive and galvanizes us to endure.

Peter tells us in 2 Peter 1:3 how God's power gives us everything we need for a godly life. In verses 5-7, Peter urges us to supplement our faith with moral excellence, knowledge, self-control, patient endurance, godliness, brotherly affection, and love. He says, "the more you grow like this, the more productive and useful you will be in your knowledge of our Lord Jesus Christ" (2 Peter 1:8 NLT). As we grow spiritually, our faith will increase, and we can avoid ineffectiveness in the work Jesus has called us to do. The result will be a useful and fruitful life.

Peter urges us to not be stagnant but to continue to grow. Even in our old age, God wants us to increase in wisdom and our knowledge of Him, investing both in the next generations. As you study the Bible and seek wisdom, ask God to fortify you with renewed vision and energy. Grow and maintain your effectiveness for the gospel by allowing the Holy Spirit to mature you in the ways Peter describes.

Dear Lord, I want to be alive in your Spirit. Teach me how to walk with Jesus and galvanize me for your purposes. Show me how to remain productive and fruitful until the day you take me home. Amen.

50
Perspective

For my thoughts are not your thoughts, neither are your ways my ways, declares the Lord. As the heavens are higher than the earth, so are my ways higher than your ways and my thoughts than your thoughts (Isaiah 55:8-9 NIV).

The day my son trimmed tree limbs with a chain saw sixty feet in the air, my heart did more than a few flip-flops. High in the bucket lift, Andrew could see the farmhouse, the campsite area, and the treetops from a vantage point I will never have. Because I will never by bet or threat get in that bucket.

I am content to safely stand on the dam where I can view the pond and maybe catch a stunning sunset. I can also look down from the dam to the farmhouse, where children and dogs chase balls and each other.

No matter how high we can get by standing on the dam, climbing a tree, or riding in a bucket lift, our view is limited. We might think if we could only find a higher vantage point, we would understand better and have a greater knowledge of whatever we want to see.

Then along came access to personal drones. Some of our grandsons collectively purchased a drone with a high-tech camera. Now we can watch videos of wide areas of The Farm and from a vantage point we never had before. The same view the vultures and eagles enjoy every day.

Our eyes can only see so much, leaving us longing for a fresh look with a new perspective. Even if we stood on the pinnacle of the tallest mountain in the world, peered down from the highest floor of a high-rise building or from a jumbo jet 35,000 feet in the air, we still would not have the view or understanding revealed by God in His word. He gives us the ability to see what we can't on our own.

This life does not always make sense. Some situations bring us nothing but confusion. Age-old perplexing questions often surface in our thoughts and conversations: Why do bad things happen? When will this end? How can it possibly work out for good? Though life is sometimes difficult to understand, God offers the perspective we desire. Jesus told us life would be hard (John 16:33), but the Bible also tells us God rules the world, and we will see His grace at work bringing about good (Romans 8:28). We can run to Him for comfort and perspective (Deuteronomy 31:6, Psalm 84:11).

In Luke 12:32, Jesus assured His disciples, "Fear not, little flock, for it is your Father's good pleasure to give you the kingdom." If through our adoption into His family we are now heirs of the kingdom, we have no need to be anxious about our inability to see into the future. Rather, we are to make room for and anticipate the providence of God. He has never failed one of His own.

He has been faithful to you in the past, and you can trust Him for your future.

Dear Heavenly Father, thank you for being patient with me when I cannot fully understand your sovereign ways. I want to yield to your higher thoughts and ways and trust you know what is best for me. Your plans are perfect. Amen.

51
Unseen

> The wind blows where it wishes, and you hear its sound, but you do not know where it comes from or where it goes. So it is with everyone who is born of the Spirit (John 3:8).

Here on the Oklahoma prairie, the wind makes its presence known most days. In our state, we sing about "waving wheat." We have all been mesmerized by the constant motion of a field of tall grass as the wind, like an invisible hand, sweeps it back and forth. We delight in watching windmills do their work, pumping water from the ground.

When the wind is just right, the children know how to utilize it for fun. They fly their kites from the top of the dam or run through the field with their kites soaring high behind them. Occasionally, the winds are more powerful, and we might find tin roofing from a neighbor's barn dumped unceremoniously on our property.

In every case, we do not actually see the wind. We only observe its effects.

John 3 tells the story of Nicodemus, a Jewish Rabbi who secretly went to Jesus in the safety of night. Jesus explains to him how one must be born again to see the kingdom of God. When Nicodemus asked how this could happen, Jesus used the wind to illustrate the Holy Spirit's unseen work in the new birth. "The wind blows where it wishes, and you hear its sound, but you do not know where it comes from or where it goes. So it is with everyone who is born of the Spirit" (John 3:8).

Although the working of the Spirit is unseen by us, and often seems mysterious, the effects upon a life are easily visible. We see the results of the unseen work of the Holy Spirit in transformed lives, renewed marriages, and restored relationships.

The Hebrew word for spirit is *ruach* which means "wind, breath, air." Wind in motion. In Genesis 1, the ruach of God moved in the unformed matter and hovered over the waters. In creating the world, He brought about something that wasn't there before. Then God breathed His Spirit into man and brought him into existence (Genesis 2:7). Before Jesus left the earth, He gave the Spirit to His disciples. John 20:22 tells us He breathed on them and said to them, "Receive the Holy Spirit."

The Holy Spirit is not only the power for creation, but He is also the power for re-creation. In our transformation, the Holy Spirit brings about a newly-created love for God, love for the Word, love for other people. He is given to us not only to unite us to Christ and conform us to the character and will of God, but His transforming work assures us we will come into possession of our eternal inheritance.

Do others see the effect of the Holy Spirit working in us? As we take in God's Word and submit to His leading, the Spirit will give us the words to say and direct our actions. The apostle Paul instructs us in Ephesians 5:18 to "Be filled with the Spirit," and the means to doing so is found in Colossians 3:16. "Let the word of Christ dwell in you richly."

> *Dear Lord, thank you for giving me your Spirit to teach me and guide me in this earthly life. I pray others will see the hope that is within me. Amen.*

52
Heritage

Your testimonies are my heritage forever, for
they are the joy of my heart
(Psalm 119:111).

When we consider the blessings of our heritage, we're reminded of the old saying that goes something like this: "One generation plants the trees and another gets the shade." Treasuring our heritage means we not only recognize what we have received from others, but find joy in it and give thanks for it. Stan and I enjoyed a close relationship with each of our parents, and they were a significant part of our family life. We did not take for granted the blessing of them living into their eighties before the Lord took them home.

All four of our parents lived through the Great Depression and were very frugal. They hated throwing away anything because it might be useful one day. If they had a spare room, garage, basement, or barn to store "stuff," they did. My dad intentionally collected broken appliances.

"Might need a toaster part down the road," he often said. My brothers and I threw away at least a dozen broken toasters and waffle irons Dad left in his workroom.

Over time, sorting through their things and finding unique treasures has brought much joy. My grandmother's pie plate, the one she took to the county fair with her famous, ribbon-winning apple pie. Letters from our grandparents to our parents. Letters and cards our parents wrote to each other. They saved items that were meaningful to them. As we go through the tubs and boxes, we might shed a tear when recalling a sweet memory. At other times, we ask, "Why in the world did they save this?"

As much as we enjoy these items, we also discover other gifts that give us great joy when we inherit them. This heritage includes our unique sense of family identity, the sense of who we are. Our traditions, values, and the culture created in our home contribute to this identity, as well as how we think about God, and eternity, and how we express our beliefs to those we love.

According to Psalm 119:111, the testimony God recorded in the Scriptures is our eternal heritage. The testimonies of grace and mercy, of God's gift to us in His Son, Jesus, and of His faithfulness. This heritage, far greater than any gold or silver, is the heritage we want to pass on to our children, grandchildren, and generations to come (Isaiah 38:19).

Every family is planting something that those following will receive. Even if we did not receive good things from our family tree, our parents or other family members, we can commit to starting a new branch and passing on a culture of righteousness to our children and grandchildren.

Our joyful task now is to carefully guard this precious heritage and pass it on.

Dear Heavenly Father, your testimonies of faithfulness, mercy, and love sustain me. They give me joy and hope. I will remember the heritage I have been given and will be diligent to pass it on to others. Amen.

53
Stones

> But as it is, God arranged the members in the
> body, each one of them, as he chose
> (1 Corinthians 12:18).

Sometimes, our friends ask the funniest questions.

"Do you have any rocks at your farm?"

I stifle a snicker. "Hmmm. Yes, lots. Hundreds, thousands, millions."

Rocks of all shapes, sizes, and composites cover The Farm. They emerge from hillsides, form ridges, lay loose and at random on the ground. Before mowing, we do a walk-around to check for wayward rocks that seemingly come out of nowhere to destroy the mower blades.

For some time, Stan had wanted to create a divider between the designated parking area and the front yard. We noticed people who were unfamiliar with our desire to separate the areas tended to encroach on the lawn. He wanted to install a picket fence, but time constraints forced him to choose another way to accomplish the same thing. What about a visual barrier of evenly-spaced large stones?

One morning while reading on the front porch, I heard the tractor coming up the road. When it rounded the corner, I noted the bucket raised high. Stan stopped at his imaginary picket fence line, lowered the bucket, and dumped out several large fifty-to-sixty-pound stones. He said he found them at the original homestead where they had been used for the foundation.

Closer inspection revealed tool marks. Someone, most likely a quarryman, had fashioned the stones with a certain project in mind. They were chiseled and hewed, each with distinguishing marks left by the mason, possibly as an identifying signature. Forever, these stones will bear the marks of the quarryman.

More than one hundred years ago, the stones were selected for a specific purpose, laid out according to a cornerstone, and strategically placed as part of a structure designed by the builder. After being fitted together as tightly as possible, the stones were mortared into place, bonding them together for the strength of the entire structure. Are there any things more ordinary than rocks and stones?

When the Architect and Builder of the church began His work, He went about selecting stones for this most glorious project. He set Jesus Christ as the chief cornerstone, the One to whom everything else in eternity is oriented. Then God chose stones of His liking among His creations, carefully selecting them for His purposes.

They weren't perfect when He selected them and lifted them out of the ground. They needed hewing, shaping, and fashioning with hammers and chisels. They needed to be sanctified. Each stone was chosen for a particular spot and placed purposefully and perfectly.

1 Peter 2:5 says, "You yourselves like living stones are being built up as a spiritual house, to be a royal priesthood, to offer spiritual sacrifices acceptable to God through Jesus Christ." After selecting us for His living temple, God fashions us with care, love, and a sense of what He is building.

He bonds us together to create a structure that not only gives glory to Himself but brings blessing to others.

Forever, we will bear the marks of the Quarryman.

Thank you, Father, for choosing me. In your plan, you fashioned me and bonded me to others for your purposes, mortaring us together with the love of Christ. Thank you that we have Jesus Christ as the cornerstone, to whom everything else in this life is oriented. Amen.

> God is a specialist at making something useful and beautiful of something broken and confused.
>
> **-Charles R. Swindoll**

54
Freedom

For freedom Christ has set us free; stand firm therefore, and do not submit again to a yoke of slavery (Galatians 5:1).

On nice weather days, the rocking chairs on the back porch call our names. Sometimes Stan and I talk, sometimes we rest and listen to to the sounds around us. When grandchildren are at The Farm, happy squeals may float up from the trampoline in the camp area below us. The kitchen door bangs shut behind us when a few kids bound out of the house and run down the hill. Others might ask if they can walk to the corral to feed Jazz some apples. When Stan gives a thumbs up, they skip off, anxious for the next adventure.

The children's happiness at The Farm is impossible to miss. We sometimes describe them as "leaping like calves from the stall" (Malachi 4:2). They feel a sense of freedom to do what they enjoy. They run from one activity to another, choosing to jump on the trampoline, swing on tree swings, or play kickball on the front lawn. They may even decide to curl up inside and read a good book.

We want the grandchildren to have fun and to be safe. They are given freedom to choose from many activities while abiding within the rules of safety we laid out for them. With freedom comes responsibility. The children could be endangered if we offered no rules or if they disregarded the rules we established for their protection.

For the Christian, freedom in Christ does not mean complete autonomy. Just as the grandchildren can't do *anything* they want to do, nor can we. The "have fun and be safe" line applies to believers, as well. Freedom is simply choosing a master, and we belong to whichever master we obey, righteousness or unrighteousness. We can't serve two masters at the same time. It is neither wise nor prudent to disregard the protection God offers us when we believe and obey Him.

Through Christ's redemptive work, we have been set free from sin and darkness (2 Corinthians 3:17). Freedom from sin does not mean we're doomed to a boring, restrictive existence. Being a Christian does not cramp our lifestyle. On the contrary, it means we can have victory over a life of disobedience, regret, and shame. John 8:36 says, "If the son sets you free, you will be free indeed." May we recognize our freedom in Christ and not go back to slavery.

As believers we enjoy another blessing of freedom, free access to the throne of grace. Free access to our heavenly Father at all times. No matter the difficulties we face, the sorrows we experience, the sins we commit, we will not be turned away. God's great storehouse of grace is like the bank of heaven. We have freedom to draw out as many riches as we want and no promise in the Bible will be withheld.

Choose freedom in Christ. Choose righteousness and enjoy all God has provided for you within the boundaries of protection.

Have fun and be safe. God has given you all to enjoy.

Dear Lord, Thank you for rescuing me from sin and unrighteousness. Thank you for giving me free access to your throne of grace. May I live in a way that is pleasing to you. Amen.

55
Shade

For you have been a stronghold to the poor, a stronghold to the needy in his distress, a shelter from the storm and a shade from the heat (Isaiah 25:4).

From the time our grandchildren were very young, they could recite Papa Stan's First Rule of Farming: park in the shade. During Stan's teen years, he learned this rule while working for farmers and ranchers in the summertime. He experienced many opportunities to validate the admonition to park in the shade.

When the grands are in our car and we need to park, they say, "Remember the first rule of farming, Grammy." Or when I park in the shade, I hear accolades such as, "Good job, Grammy. You just did the first rule of farming."

We all know the refreshing feeling of stepping from the hot sun into the shade. Shade offers protection and refuge from harsh elements, a reprieve from the intense sunshine. There we can relax, be refreshed, and linger for a time. When outside in the heat, we need the shelter of the shade.

What causes us to seek the shelter of God's care? Perhaps we are exhausted by the urgent, the endless tasks, the busyness of life. Our minds are not at rest as we're always planning, managing, and worrying about the many things we *should* be doing. For the exhausted, God becomes the shade of rest, where we can assure ourselves of the value of our tasks, gain new strength, and move forward with confidence.

At other times, we are disheartened by the world and the foolishness of others. We're provoked by unfairness and the celebration of sin. For the provoked, God becomes the shelter for living consecrated lives, different from people who surround us. We can be assured God is using us to bring the shade of His mercy and care to others.

If we are discouraged by our own sin and selfishness, our inadequacies and failings can cause us to grieve. When we seek God as "a hiding place from the wind, a shelter from the storm, like streams of water in a dry place, like the shade of a great rock in a weary land" (Isaiah 32:2), He blesses us with the shade of forgiveness and righteousness and hope. It's here we find a new beginning for our thoughts.

Psalm 91:1 says, "He who dwells in the shelter of the Most High will abide in the shadow of the Almighty. I will say to the Lord, 'My refuge and my fortress, my God, in whom I trust.'" If we're to abide in the shadow of the Almighty, we must allow God's Word to fill our minds and direct our wills.

Let's seek a place of rest and comfort under God's protective covering. Like the kids say, "Park in the shade."

Dear Lord, though I often wander, discouraged and lost, I will remember to seek safety and comfort in your shadow, in the shade of forgiveness and hope. Amen.

56
Maintenance

*We must pay much closer attention to what
we have heard, lest we drift away from it
(Hebrews 2:1).*

Stan doesn't usually wake up in the morning at The Farm thinking about grease zerks. He seldom greets me with "Hold the breakfast. I'm excited to get out there and hit those zerks with grease."

For those who aren't mechanically minded, a grease zerk is a nozzle that directs the grease to parts in a machine that contact each other. Stan is wise enough to know if he doesn't attend to this important maintenance, the tractor and other implements will suffer. When neglected and left without the necessary lubrication, moving surfaces of bearings and bushings rust and seize up. Regular maintenance is not complicated and may involve just a few squirts of grease.

Life has a way of competing for our attention and keeping us from the routines of regular maintenance. Unfortunately, we often pay the price later when the cost is much greater to do a major repair. This is especially discouraging when regular maintenance could have prevented the breakdown. Sometimes, the scenario ends with "If only I had been more diligent to …"

When everything is running smoothly, neglecting maintenance comes easy. Scripture records for us the warning the Israelites received in the wilderness. "Take care lest you forget the Lord your God" (Deuteronomy 8:11). Later when experiencing prosperity, they disregarded God and all He had done for them. They drifted away, which takes little to no effort—the reason we love that lazy river ride at the water park. The lazy river never stops flowing. It carries us away, taking us wherever it wants. And we are content to ride along.

What does regular maintenance look like for the Christian? It always looks like faithful diligent study of our only source of growth and protection, the Scriptures. Without regular effort, we soon forget the promises, as well as the warnings of danger. These are the unfortunate consequences of not actively maintaining our spiritual lives. Love, compassion, and wisdom will diminish when left untended. Our faith dies from neglect.

Just like the machinery at The Farm needs consistent attention—and may even require a few shots of grease—we must attend to our spiritual maintenance. Despite God's faithfulness to us, we sometimes forget Him. But just as He did with the Israelites, God has proven Himself over and over with us. Regular fellowship with fellow believers, daily time in prayer and God's Word, and serving others will help keep our focus where it should be.

Dear Heavenly Father, I praise you for walking with me both in drought and in prosperity. I desire to maintain a daily relationship with you and never forget all you have done for me. Amen.

57
Lost

I have now seen the One who sees me
(Genesis 16:13 NIV).

How much of our lives do we spend looking for something? We may want to be reunited with our car keys, reading glasses, or the specific little wrench that will fix whatever is broken.

Stan is a very patient man, and I was never more thankful for that than when I "lost" my mom's writing desk. Mom was a faithful writer of letters, notes, and cards. I have many vivid memories of her sitting at the Queen Anne style, cherry desk penning sweet encouragement to family and friends. I thought often about carrying on her legacy of writing at this very desk.

When we moved Mom to our community, the desk came with her. With Alzheimer's disease progressing quickly, Stan and our sons moved Mom's furniture multiple times as her world shrank into smaller and smaller living spaces. Stan filled three long-term storage units to the brim with furniture from both his parents and mine. I assumed my mother's desk was in one of them.

Plans for the farmhouse included a space in our bedroom for the writing desk. A large window above the designated space looked out to the woods. When the house neared completion, I asked Stan where the desk was in the mass of furniture. He didn't know but would look for it. The patient man that he is, Stan looked for the desk several times, both in the storage buildings and in the attic. His response was always the same: "It still isn't there."

I grieved the loss of both my mother and her desk, and being the slow learner that I am, I finally turned it over to God. He knew where it was, so would He please remind me? Days later, I awakened in the night to a crazy thought. My daughter-in-law's mother had purchased some of the furniture to use at her church. Could she have bought the desk? I had no memory of putting it up for sale and no idea why I would have done so. But a few days later, we retrieved the desk from an entryway in the church, trading it for a matching table.

God is all-seeing. In Genesis 16, we find the story of Hagar, the Egyptian slave girl owned by Abram's wife, Sarai. Enslaved, mistreated, and pregnant, Hagar runs away, stopping to rest by a spring of water in the wilderness. The Lord approaches and calls her by name, telling her to return to her mistress. Hagar calls the name of the Lord, "You are a God of seeing" (Genesis 16:13). El Roi, the God who sees.

God sees the big picture and knows right where we are. His grace is sufficient, and His timing is perfect. When we feel neglected or invisible, lost or misplaced, we can be assured El Roi knows every detail of our circumstance. No matter what happens in our lives or how far we run, we are never lost to Him. He will seek us out and extend His mercy, strengthen us, and give us renewed hope.

I praise you, El Roi. Thank you for seeing me and knowing me. I will never be lost while I am in your care. Amen.

58
Grace

The Lord waits to be gracious to you, and therefore he exalts himself to show mercy to you (Isaiah 30:18).

Stan whispered and motioned me to join him at the windows, "Come look at this." I peeked around my husband to see what he found so interesting. The west side of the upstairs game room gave us a panoramic view of the trees. Ten to twelve small songbirds lined up on a tree branch, fluttering their wings in the drops of water falling all around them.

The clear blue sky indicated no sign of rain. So earlier, Stan had set up an oscillating sprinkler to water the parched grass in the back lawn. As the water approached, the birds twittered in excitement. Then the shower of water angled across the branch, drenching them again with a spontaneous, unexpected gift. When the water moved away, the birds extended their wings, fluffed their feathers, and shook so the droplets splashed freely all over them.

The birds looked identical, apparently a small flock. I did not know what they were; of course, Stan knew. "Cedar waxwings," he said. "They're very social and travel together. And they love water."

Though we might love to control the rain with a turn of the knob, we know we can do nothing to prevent it or make it happen. Rain comes at God's discretion. Ezekiel 34:26 tells us God will "send down the showers in their season; they shall be showers of blessing."

God's grace is like rain. Undeserved, unmerited, spontaneous divine favor. It is offered because God longs to be gracious to His people. In Isaiah 30:18-33, the author assures the suffering Hebrews they will weep no more and soon their brooks will run with water. The Lord will bind up the brokenness of His people and heal the wounds of the afflicted. "You shall have a song as in the night when a holy feast is kept, and gladness of heart" (Isaiah 30:29).

How can we receive this blessed grace? We need only ask. "Let us then with confidence draw near to the throne of grace, that we may receive mercy and find grace to help in time of need" (Hebrews 4:16).

Are you weary? Are you hurting physically or overwhelmed with life's demands? Ask God to shower His grace on you. Stand on the branch and joyfully receive the blessing of His comfort and care. Just as the water cleansed and refreshed the cedar waxwings, allow God's grace to cleanse and refresh you.

Grace like rain. Showers of blessing.

Dear Lord, I draw near to your throne of grace, seeking your mercy. Shower me with your blessings that I may be cleansed and refreshed. May my response to your grace be a heart of gratitude. Amen.

For all his resplendent glory and dazzling holiness, his supreme uniqueness and otherness, no one in human history has ever been more approachable than Jesus Christ.

-Dane Ortlund

59
Tethered

> I cling to you; your strong right hand holds me securely (Psalm 63:8 NLT).

If you have ever wondered how to lead a horse away, it is quite simple. Loose the horse from whatever is holding it. Then you can lead him anywhere you want him to go.

When we take Jazz out of the corral for a walk, he may think he is being set free, but he is merely being led away by something or someone else. He trades one restriction for another.

It's a simple thought, but when applied to humans it is a truism with profound consequence. A horse can't untie itself, but we can untie ourselves. Unfortunately, our nature is to wander off.

Think for a moment about what happened to Eve. She bound herself to God as her source of protection and guidance. She trusted Him. Satan, the great deceiver, wanting to lead her away, first loosed her from

God's instruction (Genesis 3:1-6). He knew Eve wanted to follow her desires. He merely helped her untie herself from God's guidance. His goal was to make Eve believe she was being held hostage. Though Eve thought she was being set free, she only traded one master for another.

Through the deceiver's suggestions and insinuations, Eve decided God was not good. How could He be good? He forbade what she desired. This is the pattern of broken reasoning mankind has continued to follow, with disastrous results. We want what we want and reason how freedom will get us what we want. And we convince ourselves that in God's outdated guidance, He does not have our best interests in mind. So, we willingly untie ourselves from a place of safety and either wander off or are led away.

Anyone who tries to untie us from our foundation, from the truth, does not have our best interest in mind. Lots of things can lead us away from what we know to be true. The loud voices of the culture talk to us and to our children every day, in an attempt to loosen us from love and trust. The first tactic is always to question the Word of God, by causing us to doubt His goodness.

We are tethered to our Creator by love, and this is where our protection begins. God's great love for us and His promise to hold us securely, as well as our love for Him and gratefulness for saving us. Jesus tells us, "You shall love the Lord your God with all your heart and with all your soul and with all your mind" (Matthew 22:37). As our love for God grows, we are bound more securely to Him.

Let's not release our grip on God's strong right hand, wander off, or be led astray. Learn to love God's Word. Remember, being tethered to the truth will keep you safe. Stand on the firm foundation of what is right and have confidence God will protect you.

Jesus assures us, "No one is able to snatch them out of the Father's hand" (John 10:29). No one can lead a tethered horse away.

Dear Father, when I untie myself from the protection of your love and attempt to make my own way, please bring me back into a relationship with you. I want to cling to you and feel your strong right hand holding me tight. Keep me tethered to your truth. Amen.

60
Anticipation

> Stay dressed for action and keep your lamps burning, and be like men who are waiting for their master to come home from the wedding feast, so that they may open the door to him at once when he comes and knocks
> (Luke 12:35-36).

Early in our marriage, we finished graduate school and welcomed our first son. We planned to move to another city to work with a campus ministry, but Stan needed some temporary work until we moved. Stan's dad had a big list of projects he needed done at The Farm, so he hired Stan to help him.

The first job was to fix a road over the creek washed out by storms. Downed trees and limbs needed to be cut up and hauled away. Stan moved stones and spread gravel. He worked hard, both by hand and with the tractor. Though hot and sweaty, Stan did not take a break. He wanted to be found working when his dad came over the hill. Not sitting under a tree sipping iced tea. Not napping in the shade.

Now when Stan and I sit on the farmhouse porch in the shade with our iced tea waiting for our children to come home, we laugh at ourselves. When we hear a car on the gravel road from the horse corral to the house, one of us says, "Here they come."

We anticipate their visit and can hardly wait until they arrive. We prepare for them, getting their bedrooms ready, stocking up on groceries and drinks, and preparing meals. We are ready for them, watching and waiting with lots of cookies.

The car barely stops before the doors fly open. Children and dogs pile out and run about, exuberant and full of joy.

While we anxiously awaited their arrival, they looked forward to being at The Farm, with all the freedom, fun, and joy they experience being with us and the cousins.

As hard as we work to impress our boss or prepare for company in our homes, are we ready to welcome Jesus when He returns? Anticipating Christ's return in the future is the foundation of our joy here on earth. "I will come again and will take you to myself, that where I am you may be also" (John 14:3). All we desire and hope for will be found in Jesus when He comes for us.

The apostle Peter wrote in 2 Peter 3:13-14, "According to his promise we are waiting for new heavens and a new earth in which righteousness dwells. Therefore, beloved, since you are waiting for these, be diligent to be found by him without spot or blemish, and at peace." Blessed are those servants whom the master finds awake when He comes. Let's watch for the Lord to return, as a servant watches for his master. When He knocks, we will open the door to Him and rejoice.

Oh Lord, teach me how to have joy today, how to be heavenly minded, and how to have hope for the future. I want to do your work and be ready to joyfully greet you when you return. Amen.

In Closing

Thank you, friends, for joining me at The Farm.

I pray while you study God's Word, you continue to grow in knowledge of the triune God and, as a result, learn to love Him more. As the apostle Paul encouraged the Ephesians, "I pray that out of his glorious riches he may strengthen you with power through his Spirit in your inner being, so that Christ may dwell in your hearts through faith" (Ephesians 3:16-17 NIV).

Unlike the temporal doors to the farmhouse, Jesus Christ is the door to life everlasting (John 10:9). All of us must begin our relationship with Jesus by coming to Him. He gladly receives us. He is the Rescuer.

Blessings to you as you walk with God in the days and years to come.

~Cheryl

RECIPES FROM THE FARM

Great-Grandma's Old-Fashioned Pull-A-Parts

Pull-a-parts were one of Grandma Heylin's many claims to fame. Each visitor felt as if she made these tasty treats just for them.

Dough Ingredients

    1 stick (½ cup) butter, room temperature
    1 cup milk
    ½ cup sugar
    3 eggs, room temperature and beaten
    1 teaspoon salt
    2 packages active dry yeast (4 teaspoons)
        dissolved in ½ cup warm water
    4-5 cups all-purpose flour

Dipping Ingredients

    1 cup sugar
    1 teaspoon cinnamon
    1 stick (½ cup) butter, melted

Prepare round cake pans by brushing them with butter. Or, prepare a metal bundt cake pan by brushing with melted butter.

Warm the first 3 ingredients to steaming in a saucepan over medium flame. Cool to about 100°F and then pour the liquid into a large mixing bowl. Stir in eggs, salt and dissolved yeast in water.

Add flour, 1 cup at a time, until the dough becomes pliable and manageable. Cover and let dough rise to double. Once doubled in size, punch down, stir and roll out on a floured surface into a 10"x18" rectangle.

Cut rolled out dough into ½"- 1" squares. In a medium bowl, combine 'dipping ingredients'. Dip the squares into the dipping mixture, coating all sides and then place into the prepared pan(s). Let rise.

Preheat oven to 350°. When the pull-a-parts have doubled in size, bake until browned and done in the middle. Serves 8-10.

Grammy's Famous Frozen Cookies (GFFCs)

Whether we're home or traveling, at least two dozen of these cookies must be present in my freezer at all times. When the grandchildren come to visit, they give hugs then head to the freezer to grab a GFFC.

    2 sticks butter, softened
    ¾ c white sugar
    ¾ c brown sugar, packed
    2 eggs
    2 teaspoons pure vanilla extract
    1 ½ cup flour
    1 teaspoon baking soda
    1 teaspoon kosher salt

Add:
3 cups old fashioned oats
2 cups chocolate chips

Preheat oven to 350°.

Using a stand mixer, cream together butter and sugars.

Add eggs and vanilla and continue mixing until fully incorporated into the butter/sugar mixture, scraping the sides after one minute.

Next, add the flour, baking soda, salt and oats. Mix on low-speed until the flour and oats are incorporated (scraping the sides and bottom to completely combine). Pour in the chocolate chips and mix gently on low until evenly distributed.

Drop the cookie dough by heaping teaspoons on ungreased cookie sheet. Bake for 9-11 minutes (or to your desired doneness). Remove from the oven when lightly browned. Let the cookies rest for one minute, then move them to cooling racks.

Makes 4 dozen.

When cool, place in freezer bags and keep in freezer.

Alice's Cranberry Salad

This beautiful, fluffy, tangy "salad" is the perfect addition to your Christmas feasts. The perfect bite? A little piece of roasted turkey smooshed together with sage stuffing topped off with a dollop of Alice's Cranberry Salad. It's a dreamy, comforting mouthful!

- 1 pound fresh cranberries
- 1 pound red grapes, sliced in half
- ¾ cup sugar
- ½ pint (8 ounces) heavy whipping cream, whipped*
- 1 cup chopped pecans
- 1 ½ cups miniature marshmallows

Using a food processor, grind the cranberries, pulsing to reduce the cranberries to a fine chop stage.

Place the finely-chopped cranberries into a medium mixing bowl and stir in the sugar. Cover and refrigerate cranberry mixture overnight.

Six to eight hours later (or the next day), drain and discard the liquid from the cranberries. Fold in the grapes, whipped cream, pecans and marshmallows.

Place the salad into a serving bowl and refrigerate 1 to 2 hours.

*Note: Whip the heavy whipping cream after the cranberry/sugar mixture has refrigerated 6-8 hours.

Serves 10-12.

Cheese Grits

Cheese grits are an Independence Day family tradition and a familiar side at The Farm. We enjoy it served alongside grilled teriyaki skewers, but this dish is also perfect for anything barbeque.

- 1 ½ cups grits, original
- 6 cups water
- 2 teaspoons kosher salt
- ½ teaspoon pepper
- 3 eggs, beaten
- 1 lb. Velveeta, diced into 1" cubes
- ½ cup cold butter, sliced into 8-10 pats
- ¼ teaspoon Tabasco (optional, for a little kick)

Preheat the oven to 350° and prepare a 9"x13" baking dish by buttering the bottom and all sides.

In a 4–6-quart soup pot, bring the water to a boil. Once the water is boiling, add the grits to the water, reduce the heat to low and stir continuously for 5 minutes.

After five minutes, temper the eggs with the hot grits by spooning 3-4 tablespoons of the grits into the beaten eggs. Stir quickly to prevent the egg from scrambling and then pour the egg mixture into the grits.

Add the remaining ingredients, continuing to stir over low heat until the cheese and butter are melted. Place the grits into the prepared baking dish and bake for 40-50 minutes or until the top is lightly browned.

Serves 12.

Variations:

Explore with other cheeses. Remove 4 ounces of Velveeta and replace it with 4 ounces of smoked gouda or blue cheese for a unique side.

Gram's Holiday Cheese Ball

If you've had the opportunity to experience Gram's hugs or Gram's Holiday Cheese Ball, you know just how special this lady is. This simple cheese ball is most often enjoyed with club crackers.

> 8 ounces cream cheese, softened
> 3 Tbsp sweet onion, finely minced
> 1/3 cup blue cheese crumbles
> 3/4 cup pecans or walnuts, chopped

Garnish: 2 red and 2 green maraschino cherries (optional)

In a medium bowl, stir together the first 3 ingredients. Once evenly combined, scoop the cheese mixture onto a 14" square of plastic wrap and form into a ball, wrapping tightly.

Place the wrapped cheeseball into the refrigerator for 2 hours up to overnight.

When ready to serve, place chopped nuts on a 14" square of wax or parchment paper and then place the cheese ball atop the chopped nuts. Roll the cheese ball in nuts until coated.

Serve immediately or wrap and refrigerate.

Optional: Gram's finishing touch. Cut a couple red and green maraschino cherries to make a poinsettia flower on the top of the cheese ball.

Serve with crackers.

Optional: Add ½ cup sharp cheddar cheese, shredded.

Hot Onion Soufflé

This yummy hot onion dip shows up often at family gatherings.

12 ounces cream cheese, softened
½ cup mayo
2 cups sweet onion, minced
1 cup parmesan cheese, grated

Preheat oven to 350°. Prepare a 9"x 6" baking dish by spraying with nonstick cooking spray.

In a medium mixing bowl, combine ingredients, stirring to mix thoroughly.

Place the dip mixture into the prepared dish and spread evenly.

Bake for 30 minutes or until bubbly and lightly browned.

Serve with a variety of crackers.

Optional: Experiment with other white cheeses.

Notes

1. Demoss, Nancy Leigh. Choosing Gratitude: Your Journey to Joy (Chicago, IL: Moody Press, 2009), 29.
2. Stanley, Charles F., and Charles F. Stanley. Charles Stanley's Handbook for Christian Living: Biblical Answers to Life's Tough Questions (Nashville, TN: Thomas Nelson, 2008), 193.
3. Spurgeon, Charles H. Morning and Evening (Wheaton, IL: Crossway Books, 2003), June 28 Morning.
4. Tada, Joni Eareckson. Heaven: Your Real Home (Grand Rapids, MI: Harper Collins, 1997), 53.
5. Spurgeon, Charles H. Morning and Evening (Wheaton, IL: Crossway Books, 2003), June 3 Morning.
6. Grant County Historical Society, History of Grant County Families (Grant County Historical Society Inc., 1980), 202-203.
7. Lewis, C.S. "They Asked for a Paper," Is Theology Poetry? (London: Geoffrey Bless, 1962), 164-165.
8. Spurgeon, Charles H. Morning and Evening (Wheaton, IL: Crossway Books, 2003), February 16 Morning.
9. Swindoll, Charles R. Start Where You Are (Nashville, TN: Thomas Nelson, 1999), 11.
10. Ortlund, Dane. Gentle and Lowly (Wheaton, IL: Crossway, 2020), 20.

Acknowledgments

When I began writing this devotional, I never dreamed how it would challenge me as a writer and how much I would learn. I must acknowledge many people, without whom this book would not exist.

I must first thank my husband, Stan Schuermann, for his continual encouragement. His faithful prayer kept me going when I doubted. Stan studied the Scriptures with me, always ready and willing to talk through the theological truths. His artistic talent displayed in the illustrations brought *Farmhouse Devotions* to life and made the book everything I dreamed it could be.

My heart overflows with thankfulness for my children and grandchildren, the inspiration and the energy behind this book. These beautiful people are the stories behind the stories. All my love to David and Emily, Kade, Brody, Shepard, Ava Grace; Matt and Tana, Joel, Abbie, Caleb; Andrew and Leslie, Claire, Hannah; Daniel and Marcy, Amelia, Norah, June, and Max Henry. An additional thank you to daughter-in-law Emily of Food for a Year for lending her professional expertise in reviewing the recipes.

A heartfelt thank you goes to Ava Pennington and the members of my Word Weavers Page 38 and Page 54 critique groups. Your excellent critiques have made me a better writer. Thank you for your wise counsel and encouragement.

To Rhonda Rhea and Karen and George Porter at Bold Vision Books who first believed in this project and gave my proposal a "Yes." To Shellie Arnold at Kaleidoscope Publishing, you have blessed me by bringing me into the Kaleidoscope family with talented authors, editors, and production staff, to give my book new life. I am forever thankful for this opportunity.

To Larry J. Leech II, my outstanding first edition editor at Bold Vision Books. You made my manuscript sparkle with your insightful editing. Thank you.

I am grateful to those who thoughtfully endorsed this book and to those who blessed my launch team with your energy. I could not have done it without you. Thank you for promoting *Farmhouse Devotions* and for all your kind comments on social media and in reviews. I pray this book will encourage you for years to come.

Finally, and most importantly, I am in awe at God's grace throughout this two-year project. His patience with me never tires. His tender instruction is always perfect and opens my eyes to see His glory in the ordinary.

Meet Cheryl Schuermann

Before she began writing full-time, **Cheryl Schuermann** devoted her professional career to literacy education as a classroom teacher, consultant, and curriculum trainer in schools across the United States.

Cheryl is a president in Word Weavers International and a member of Advanced Writers and Speakers Association, Christian Authors Network/CIPA. Find her and her other books at www.cherylschuermann.com.

Retired from a professional career, **Stan Schuermann** now spends his time writing, speaking, and tackling the many chores at The Farm. An occasional artist, he enjoyed contributing to *Farmhouse Devotions* with farm-inspired artwork.

For more than twenty-five years, Stan and Cheryl have mentored and taught parents in their local church. They have four married sons and find great delight in spending time with their thirteen grandchildren, the inspiration for their many stories. The Farm is their favorite place to write, be with family, and host ministry groups.

www.ingramcontent.com/pod-product-compliance
Lightning Source LLC
Chambersburg PA
CBHW062124040426
42337CB00044B/3906